RAILROADS

AN AMERICAN JOURNEY

RAILROADS

AN AMERICAN JOURNEY

DON BALL, JR.

New York Graphic Society
Boston, Massachusetts

By the same author

PORTRAIT OF THE RAILS: FROM STEAM TO DIESEL

International Standard Book Number 0 - 316-73300-8
Library of Congress Catalog Card Number 74-78769

First published 1975 by New York Graphic Society Ltd.
11 Beacon St., Boston, Mass. 02108

Designed by Bernard Schleifer

Printed in the United States of America

To my Dad—
the best friend I ever had.
He loved life and fully lived
every moment.

BALL

CONTENTS

If Only for a Moment... 11

Introduction—The End of an Era 13

How Can I Tell Him? 17

1 My Decade 1950-1960 19

2 A Closer Look 167

3 Shortlines: Autumn Memories 191

4 Fan Fare 225

5 Changing of the Guard 253

BALL

PHOTO CREDITS

Photographic credits are listed in captions in the following sequence: left-hand page, top to bottom; right-hand page, top to bottom. Where all photographs on a page are by the same person, only one name will appear. Negatives in the author's collection are credited as "Collection."

Don Ball, Jr.	Missouri Pacific (MP)
Ray Buhrmaster	Norfolk and Western (N&W)
Joe G. Collias	Ed Nowak
Robert L. Collins	Robert P. Olmsted
T. J. Donahue	John Pickett
Howard Fogg	Phil Ronfor
Henry R. Griffiths, Jr.	Bud Rothaar
Robert Hale	Jim Shaughnessy
Victor Hand	Donald Sims
Herb Harwood	Donald E. Smith
Philip R. Hastings	Richard Steinheimer
Harley Kelso	Harold Stirton
Charles H. Kerrigan	Fletcher Swan
Franklin King	Union Pacific (UP)
Stan Kistler	John J. Wheelihan
James T. La Vake	Andy Wittenborn
O. Winston Link	Bill Wolfe
Robert R. Malinoski	Don Wood
Marsh Studios	J. J. Young
Bruce Meyer	Karl Zimmerman

IF ONLY FOR A MOMENT...

BALL

I have lived near the Atlantic Ocean for most of my life now and have come to know the wonderful sense of freedom and solitude a lonely beach can offer. Then too, traveling the length and breadth of America, I have witnessed the many changes, seen with anguish the ravished countryside—man-inflicted wounds resulting from population explosion and commercial exploitation. As a people beholding the spread of a seemingly incurable disease, we wait and watch—and wonder if at any point we can stop it before it is too late. Oh Lord, the America of my childhood is gone—but my heart is still full of its past quiet pleasures.

So often today there is that deep desire to escape . . . to get away from the constant hum of tires on the highway . . . the raucous roar of trucks and buses . . . the ubiquitous bulldozer. To get away from mammoth shopping centers . . . sprawling housing developments . . . urban decay. It is then that I return to that great Atlantic beach to watch the graceful gulls wheel and cry in their own world of sky and sea—while beneath their soaring silver wings, mile upon mile of sand and rolling dunes stretch on forever; to stand and listen to the eternal bombardment of crashing waves and the outward rush of the pebble-carrying undertow; to watch the silent fog roll in—gray and ghostly—over the endless beach; and through it, to catch occasional glimpses of the tumbling ocean half hidden in the mist.

And, strangely, I can sense, in the thunder of the surf relentlessly battering the beach, the massive roar of a great steam locomotive—pounding, storming, sanding, working its way over the steel rails in a constant surge of sound—a tremendous outpouring of raw power as it thunders past, leaving skeins of steam hanging in the air, like the spindrift blowing over the beach.

If only for a moment, look at the thundering surf and listen with me . . .

BALL

INTRODUCTION–
THE END OF AN ERA

Perhaps it's inevitable that I associate my love for railroads with my love for America. We all know that America "played host" to the railroads (or did the railroads play host to America?) and that there was a time when the trains symbolized our nation's commerce and powerfully captured our imagination. Lucius Beebe talked of locomotive smoke plumes as "tangible symbols and oriflamme of a universal preoccupation with movement and the realization of a continental dimension" . . . smoke plumes that "moved with compulsive majesty across the summer horizons of a nation bound on mighty land-farings."

All of us have memories from our impressionable youth. The days of my youth were good days—days of an America I truly loved. Times of a simpler life. When I was a kid, we didn't have cars and radios, drive-ins after school, or TV's at home. Reflecting back on that time, I think of the ways we had to be resourceful at play, to make do with what little was available—and always within a ten-minute dash home for dinner! If you lived in a small town, you know whereof I speak, and if you lived in a small town with a railroad going through it, you know how grand and wonderful the railroad was. We almost always ended up playing near the railroad tracks. After all, could anything be more captivating than the great trains that came and went?

A long freight train would provide a barrel of fun and many a game for us. After gesturing "pull the whistle" to the engineer, we'd look for cars from railroads we had never heard of, see who could identify heralds first—before the car passed—and look for "Phoebe Snow" cars and "billy-goat" symbols and, of course, guess beforehand how many cars there would be. With the awesome steam locomotives, there was always that irresistible urge to put pennies on the track—if we had any. We'd see whose stayed on the longest—hoping they'd stay on for all the drivers—and whose would end up biggest. (I'd hate to think how many times I rounded up empty pop bottles to take back to the market to get more pennies for the track!)

When I was a boy, our town had brick-paved, elm-shaded streets, with big white houses. The sunshine would filter down through the trees onto the neat green lawns. On rainy days, we could stand under certain trees and stay practically dry! In back,along the alley, everyone had a garden—full of vegetables and fragrant flowers. Everything seemed so serene and orderly. At the end of the day, a big treat for the family was an evening drive "around the square." We'd all get in the old Chevy and head out west of town along the highway (we called it the slab) next to the tracks. I'd look for smoke plumes, everyone else would look at the growing fields. We'd all join in reading out loud the jaunty, story-telling Burma-Shave signs. DOES YOUR HUS-BAND/MISBEHAVE/GRUNT AND GRUMBLE/RANT AND RAVE/SHOOT THE BRUTE SOME/BURMA-SHAVE. Everyone had his favorites and would try to remember them, after new signs were put up. PITY ALL/THE MIGHTY CAESARS/THEY PULLED/EACH WHISKER OUT/WITH TWEEZERS. Whoever was in the back seat had the task of unscrambling the signs in the opposite direction! OF THEM FOR SEED/TO LEAVE ONE HALF/YOU DON'T NEED/WHISKERS/WHEN CUT-TING. Several miles west, we'd turn right on the blacktop and head north through the cornfields. Eventually we would end up along the tracks that curved to the north, then headed out east of town. A sharp right, along a dirt road, would bring us back towards town and to the depot. During the evening, it seemed that everyone came down to the depot to watch the trains. It was a social gathering, of sorts, for the women, but for the men and kids the trains were the main attraction. When it was time to go home, my only consolation was that I'd be back tomorrow!

I'm sure there isn't a kid in the world who doesn't have a secret place to go to when he wants to be alone. I know I had several. Alone the Kaw River, just below the Union Pacific-Rock Island tracks and through the buckbush, I'd have the world to myself—along with all the wild raspberries and black-berries I could eat. There were trees we called little pawpaws, along with the buckeyes and redbuds. In the springtime, the redbuds were a brilliant lav-ender against the willow green of the buckbush. In the summer, the buck-bush stayed green, in sharp contrast to the surrounding brown hues. Back along the tracks were the much taller sycamores and cottonwoods, and every-where, red-wing blackbirds fluttered overhead. The tracks were always within sight.

One summer day, I ventured many miles down the tracks and along the river. I was seven or eight years old, for I had my first Brownie box camera at the time. I made sure I stayed within hearing and running distance of the tracks. Several hours, and trains, must have passed, for I heard distant deep rumbling from out of the west. All at once the bright sunshine gave way to the fast approaching jagged edge of a dark grey thunderhead. The light quickly dulled as the sun was opaqued behind the huge cloud's silvery edge. The blue sky above quickly lost its brilliance. The air suddenly became eerily quiet. Thunder rolled again and in a moment a breeze started up. In seconds the wind came, like a fast-rushing train, turning the leaves under, white. I ran along the crossties, as I often had before. Lighting started to flash and play nearby and I ran faster. No trains were coming. Not at all too soon I arrived at the depot in the leading edge of the downpour. The lightning was ten times as blinding as before, the crashes deafening. I knew I would spend the rest of the afternoon in the shelter of the depot. The trains would still come, definitely more dramatically in the storm!

I vividly remember the great looming locomotives in the rain—whistling, approaching, clanking past the depot, rattling the windows and stomping up to the water plug. The engines seemed haughty out there in the downpour, shaking the drenching rain off their boiler jackets. Every part mirrored its shape and contour from the soaking—and I'd feel sorry for the fireboy up on the tank, putting water into the hatch. The depot was a great place to be, in the rain.

After the storm would come the clearing, the low sun breaking through the dissipating clouds, turning everything to gold. The air would be clean and cool. Birds would be singing again. Before going home, I'd wait for just one more train!

Yes, I remember that sudden thunderstorm, and being flushed like a quail from cover. For me, it was the percussion, from trackside, of a heavenly symphony and I was part of the audience to nature's performance.

I thank God for these moments—the wonderment of trains, thunder-storms, sunlight! There's so much wealth around us—free for the looking. My dad always said that my pursuit of trains gave me the great out-of-doors America. He was right, and I'm grateful for it. I'm sure every time I've waited for a train, I've enriched my life a little. And yes, I get that almost awestruck, distinctly lonely feeling that I have something special—something free for the taking, something only a few of us possess.

I recall with special vividness summer Sunday mornings in our town. Our house was just up the street from the Ninth Street Baptist Church. How I loved lying in bed, watching the people in their whitest-of-white walking along the red-brick sidewalks! How I loved the "revival" music that filled the air! The Baptists were always in church before the rest of us had even had breakfast. I'd go to Sunday School at ten and somehow would always squeeze in enough time to run down to the end of our street in the hope that Santa Fe's *Antelope*, due around 9:30, would be on time. A big 3461-class Hudson was usually on this train—the engine with the 7-foot drivers! I'd stay and watch the opposing semaphore on the single-track line and hope that it would drop to yellow. I think I got as great a thrill from the approach signal and the distant whistling as I did when that big locomotive galloped and huffed around the bend, bell ringing, drifting smoke, shaking the ground as it pounded past.

The "pocket-knife whittlin', chair-rockin', and shade-tree settin'" era is gone in America. . . . gone with the gentler sights and sounds and smells of an earlier day . . . gone the way of the quiet streets and hushed wooded land-scapes . . . gone with the Saturday nights on the square, the popcorn cart, and the steam locomotive. I think of all those wonderful things that, when we had them, we took for granted. Today's children, in all likelihood, will not know the joy of running down a crooked little road to a clear pond for tadpoles, or the fun of walking through the fragrant fields, still wet with dew, catching butterflies and grasshoppers and watching the cows clearing out for the shade of the trees. Today's children do not even have the local depot to go to, to listen to the clatter of a telegraph key and ask when the next train is due . . . and whether it's steam or diesel, freight or passenger.

Often today I'm astounded to read about something being "discovered" —and described as if whatever was "discovered" was new. For instance, I hear about the "leisure time" to be found on a long train ride, or friends tell about their drive to an apple orchard where they can pay to pick (or to wait in line to pick) their own apples, and gasoline companies offer the motorist high-way guides to the best places to view trees in the fall. No, there is little comfort in the thought of being part of this pay-for-amusement, TV and neon, drive-in-for-hamburger world.

These days, when individual joy and inventiveness are seldom seen, I simply turn to reminiscing. I like to go back and remember the skies of my boyhood. In Kansas, nothing dominated the landscape as much as the sky. Everywhere, I felt a grand affinity to it all: the land stretching out like the broad sea, the distant grain elevators standing erect, resembling far-off ships. The endless sky and horizon humbled you. At a young age I learned to forecast weather by understanding the sky's color, clouds, and winds. Take a good look at the sky someday. Get to know mares' tails and anvil-tops and find out what they mean. If a mackerel sky is evident an hour before sundown, wait around. If possible, get to a good westward vista. Pity the soul who does not wonder at the sky. Pity the empty being who is too busy coping with today's world to look up!

Even today I am not bored when I wait beside the railroad tracks. For that matter, I do not really know what boredom is. I believe that nature— whatever its form—is sustenance for my soul. I do not profess to have all the answers to the secret of happy living, but I would offer the acceptance of nature's bounty as a start. Take a look at the sky someday—a good long look. You'll be the better for it.

16

HOW CAN I TELL HIM?

BALL

Long ago, many years more than I want to recall, I stood down on those tracks below the bluffs and watched the trains. One train that lingers vividly in my memory is Union Pacific's No. 39 out of Kansas City. That big stacked Pacific held a place in my heart. Usually the 3222 or the 3221 was assigned. I liked these engines the best because they had large tenders and seemed to harmonize with the red, yellow, and grey Harriman cars. Right about there is where I'd stand. The morning light was always just right. The backlit locomotive would loom at me and swing past on the curve, high drivers and rods glinting in the sun, yellow cars obediently following around the curve, their six-wheeled trucks clicking over the rail joints. Today, the air is clear and the light is perfect . . . just as I remember it. A beautiful day to walk along the bluffs.

"Dad, are there any steam engines?"

"No, not here . . . not now."

"We'd better catch up with Mommy."

Fen reached up and took my hand and together we ran back to Linda and the car. A few minutes' drive brought us to the R. H. Long Museum and the waiting in-laws. Together we entered the museum's large hall depicting the early days of Kansas City—the arrival of steamboats and the railroad. Sounds from the past, so familiar, came from a small aperture above our heads, filling the room. The arrival of a train!

"Dad!"

Fenner ran towards the nearest window. It was frosted glass.

"Yes, Fen, we'll look when we leave."

This small son of mine who holds such a large place in my affections . . . I love him! We share a very deep and special bond—a closeness and a mutual sharing that can't be put into words. He has been and is a part of my joy in railroading too, through almost constant exposure to my model-building and photography, not to mention the pulse-quickening thunder of "stack-talk" on my innumerable recordings of steam trains. These delight him!

How can I tell him that the Nickel Plate Berkshire we chased on freight was a one-of-a-kind event—made possible by a Steamtown, a Ross Rowland, a George Leilich, and the Western Maryland? What about that moment when the same engine blasted beneath us on a Pocono grade, on freight? Sure, it was on the Erie-Lackawanna and the locomotive was making her last run, but the number 759 didn't register. What about that Reading T-1 running light on the CNJ? How can I tell him that these trackside travels were final, that we were witnessing the very end? To his way of thinking, it's all still there—and always will be.

BUT IT'S GONE!

And no matter how I might try to explain its passing, in his heart-of-hearts he just couldn't, wouldn't, believe me!

HOW CAN I TELL HIM?

BALL

Amid the deafening sound of it all, the fireman somehow made himself heard, leaning way out from his high perch up in the cab. "Hey! Take a picture of me!" Well, that's exactly what I did, hoping he was back in the cab when I clicked the shutter just as the engine was about to pass. Anyway, with almost 130 feet of locomotive and tender, sixteen working drivers, and all the machinery a plumber could ask for, who could possibly notice the fireman? Besides, that beautiful plume of tumbling smoke took up most of the picture. It was well worth the two-hour trackside wait. After the endless train of empty hopper cars passes, I'll head for Flushing tunnel and give that fireman another chance. In a long procession, the following black hoppers sing and sway around the curve—their wheels banging away at the rail joints in beautifully repetitious rhythm—their loose journal-box lids clinking and clanking through the West Virginia hills in a symphony of steel. Up front (on the head end) that well-proportioned, massive EM-1 articulated tells me what it's all about, working her train with a vengeance, climbing the mountains back towards the mines—each exhaust booming up toward the heavens and echoing through the hills, her steamboat whistle now clearing the grade crossings in a small settlement a mile up the track. I dutifully jotted down "B & O EM-1 #7605 - Benwood to Holloway - Barton, W/Va. 5-29-55. Tri-x F-11 1/250 sec." in my small black notebook. The caboose finally appeared around the bend, slowly approached, and passed. For the next two weeks, I would live in a wonderful world of trains! This was my annual end-of-summer "high-iron heyday," and the rails were loaded with almost everything I wanted to see!

No doubt about it—1955 was my favorite railroad year, and it marked the middle of *my* railroad decade. The 1950's were too late in the railroad adventure for many, but for me, these ten years offered the most exciting, colorful, and treasured experiences of all. Consider, if you will: in 1950 the diesel had made its mark . . . had finally dealt a fatal blow to the reciprocating steam locomotive. But consider also . . . that 1950 was a year that found B&O's top-performance champion, the *Cincinnatian*, still drawn by steam; that steam and gas turbines were coming off the drawing boards and into service; that Roanoke was still building reciprocating steam, while at Crestline, Ohio, Pennsy had shoved its steam turbine into the weeds and chalked up "scrap" next to "#6200" on the enginehouse assignment board. Consider too that EMD had entered its final stage of E-unit production; that self-propelled diesel rail cars had made branchline inroads, while in the mid-50's, low-slung, quite unorthodox lightweight trains were meeting with railroad and public favor. I make no apologies—1950 to 1960 was *the* decade of train-watching for me!

I've had a joyous obsession with trains since childhood. Maybe I should say, with railroading. I always had my favorites—Santa Fe, Rock Island, Union Pacific, Missouri Pacific, B&O, New York Central, New Haven. During "my decade" I loved these railroads for their locomotives, their trains, and yes, even their paint schemes when the diesels came.

In the early part of my decade, each railroad, to me, had its own distinct individuality. The Union Pacific was reefer blocks . . . an endless fast-moving train of orange and yellow cars, following from under the rolling smoke-canopy of a pencil-boilered locomotive. Missouri Pacific meant well-proportioned locomotives, each with a neat and purposeful look. Missouri Pacific's lettering was conservative, while the numbers were functionally large for easy identification, and the diesel-powered Eagle streamliners were in the best of taste—original, distinctive—a beautiful variation in the course of train-watching along the MoP. The Rock Island, like the MoP, had a stable of beautifully proportioned steamers. The large red herald emblazoned on the tenders was a symbol of positive identification to the general public, a symbol of pride to me. Their diesels were perhaps my favorites. One word characterizes the Rock's crimson, maroon, and silver trains: smart. The Santa Fe's passenger trains were the embodiment of speed. Slant-nosed diesel pacers with the striking red-and-yellow "war-bonnet" paint scheme—peculiarly fitting for the awesome, flat, great Southwest through which they sped. In the early days of diesels, it was hard not to be enchanted with the Santa Fe. Its modern steamers were all from the same perfectly proportioned Baldwin mold. Great, strong locomotives suited to the vast distances they covered. And I loved their hallmark stack-extensions! They added a towering feeling to the locomotive's already awesome dimensions.

Back East, where cities are closer and geography more restrictive and varied, the railroad was almost obtrusive. It seemed that each road's property was highly visible, everywhere evidenced by the operation of "drills," locals, and "ordinaries"—or RDCs and MUs. When and where a train wasn't visible, it seemed there was always a siding with a boxcar or gon belonging to the local carrier. Pennsy seemed to be everywhere, an iron-and-steel giant! Under wires, through the mountains, out in the farmlands—the great keystone connoted its strength. New York Central ... the great New York Central (someone once called it "the princely New York Central") ... always impressed me as being a business showcase. Efficient and profitable, as a Vanderbilt would have it. The Hudson locomotive was the embodiment of New York Central: graceful, clean-lined, limber, fleet. The Mohawk, the logical outgrowth of the Hudson—was ideally suited for heavy passenger assignments and fast water-level freights. The Niagara was a classic example of utility —that is, with everything engineered that could possibly be engineered within the clearance restrictions of New York Central. The B&O? Ah, that's another story: The Mother of Railroads, steeped in tradition; a friend, a neighbor to the states it served; a railroad whose steam locomotives—from 0-6-0's to 2-8-8-4's—had classic charisma, and whose royal blue, gold, and grey diesels carried on the distinctive family heritage. Certainly the B&O was my personal favorite in the East. Finally, there was the New Haven—impressive from the train window with its 4-track mainline under catenary that was built to last forever and its great electric engines surging countless trains under the triangular wires. Sleek new diesels from Alco, whisking stainless steel along the shoreline. And, yes, the last of the thinning ranks of fearsome, mean-looking, beetle-browed 4-8-2's and 2-10-2's on freight, and recent memories of the clean, streamlined I-5 Hudsons on some of the passenger runs ... and ... and the many (far too many) branch lines feeding off the shoreline. New Haven seemed to be a compact giant whose rails held a little of everything for the train-watcher—although it was a trail-blazing, diesel-operating renegade—by the beginning of my decade.

By mid-1960, mainline steam was memory. Memory ... as Webster defines it, *an image or impression of someone or something remembered; the time within which past events can be or are remembered.* That's it, nothing more ... memory. In mid-1960, the land could have been combed for steam—everywhere—to no avail. Rusting water columns stood alongside deserted coaling docks ... silent. And on many out-of-the-way, hard-to-get-to tracks, rows of silent, boarded-up, white-lined steamers slept away their final hours. An era had quietly passed.

In 1950, the beginning of my decade, Illinois Central's president, Wayne A. Johnston, quoted in the *Chicago Journal of Commerce*, routinely stated that the I.C. "will not dieselize its freight services for a long time, if ever." And if you were lucky enough to be around his railroad, those beautiful 4-8-2's and 2-10-2's pounded home his claim. That was 1950. By 1960? Well, a *decade* had passed.

Somehow, in my railroad world of steam, Monon and Gulf Mobile & Ohio dieselized unnoticed. Their "d-days" simply passed unsighted—as important events often do. Since I could go over to the U.P. depot and get a full line-up of steam, little else mattered. In 1952, the New Haven dieselized. Somehow, it was just meant to be. New Haven's steam locomotives with the exception of ten 4-6-4's, were old, and their time had come. I was aboard New Haven's last steam trip on April 27, 1952, and the gloomy weather precluded really getting out at trackside to look. Perhaps that was for the best. A year later—1953—Southern dieselized—on June 17, to be exact. News of Southern's "d-date" *did* appear in the press and made interesting reading. Southern, though, like Monon and GM&O, was far away and did not affect *my* railroad world. In 1954, Fairbanks Morse saturated the print media with a campaign aimed at putting an end to steam-locomotive maintenance. In the same year, Roanoke turned to a coal-fired steam turbine to power traction motors on an otherwise 100 per cent reciprocating steam-powered railroad. The story should have sunk in by then.

Although late in the game of dieselization, 1954 was the year of reckoning for me. It was in 1954 that *Trains* magazine arrived in the mail with a "steam—where to find it" article, and I noted the glaring omissions. It was also in 1954, in April, that I returned to Lawrence to visit, during spring vacation. At the first opportunity (most likely the first hour I was there!), I headed over to the U.P. depot for a look at my first 4-12-2 since the previous summer. Yellow diesels—hordes of them—bleated at the crossings and on through town. In the station, I was told, "The nines left the division, almost overnight." An awful emptiness crept into the depot with me. The combination of anxiety and disbelief, plus the weight of all those steam-filled years, was painfully immense. I felt I was at a funeral parlor. For the first time in my life, this charmed depot of my boyhood was an empty facade. The land I loved was suddenly different . . . quiet, deserted. The green screen door to the waiting room slammed shut behind me. Across the tracks, someone was burning freshly raked, damp, musty leaves from last fall. The pungency of the smoke made an unforgettable ceremonial incense. I knew this was the day I would close and board up my boyhood Lawrence.

The warm spring sun shone on the rails. Lavender flowers with tiny yellow centers clustered together next to the right of way. I walked down to the end of the platform to the water plug and looked at the slip marks burned into the rails by steam locomotives. Plant life had begun to sprout between the rails next to the plug, but now was fast dying from lack of water and too much sun. I took one more look down the rails—the shiny, strong rails that had always brought the great trains into Lawrence. Now, for the first time, I looked down the tracks and realized they also led *out* of town.

INK

Up to the end of steam, the Canadian National and the Canadian Pacific operated a complete representation of steam locomotive development in Canada. These three scenes from the mid-50's are typical of everyday Canadian steam railroading right up to dieselization. Above, the fire is cleaned on one of CNR's U-4-a class streamlined 4-8-4's at Turcot roundhouse in Toronto; while below, a CNR 2-8-0 heads a local freight west through deep forests near Victoria, B.C. At right, CPR's quick-stepping Pacific #2408 bounds through the spans over the St. Lawrence River as it nears Vaudreuil, Quebec. (BALL, HARWOOD, PICKETT)

Surrounding the activity and ferment of New England railroading, there was the ever-present charm of the land itself. A car of milk for Boston is switched onto the morning run at Waterbury, Vt., on the Central Vermont, while to the northeast, a Canadian Pacific 4-6-2 and 4-6-4 highball through the placid Maine countryside. Below, Montreal-bound passenger train No. 17 crosses Back Cove just out of Portland, Maine. The water is like a millpond, as the natives would say. (SHAUGHNESSY, HASTINGS, HASTINGS)

A CNR 2-8-2 gets under way on a cold winter morning out of White River Jct., Vt., while above, on a hazy warm Indian summer day, the southbound *Alouette* glides downgrade through West Burke, Vt., behind a CPR 4-6-2. At right, one of Rutland's three sightly 4-8-2's sounds her approach whistle, drifting fast into Center Rutland with the *Green Mountain Flyer* from Montreal. (BALL, HASTINGS, PICKETT)

Several hundred returning campers spend their last night together until next summer. Boston & Maine's big Pacific #3710 has brought the New York-bound special down from Maine to Worcester, Mass., where the New Haven takes over to New York City. Not-so-well-maintained Alco DL-109 #0751 and a mate will power the train as far as New Haven, Ct. At left and above, scenes from the last week of steam operations on the B&A. Hudson-type #601, alone in the world of growlers at Back Bay Station, Boston, and big Mohawk #3005 on B & A's last through steam run, heading the *Southwestern Limited* through Framingham, Mass. (HASTINGS, COLLECTION, COLLECTION)

From fame to legend, the lovely clipper ships sailed out of Boston: the *Flying Cloud,* the *Northern Light,* the *Dreadnought.* New Haven's *Yankee Clipper,* each car bearing the name of a clipper ship, sails down Sharon hill behind the flat bow of PA #0765, itself now legend. On the right page, the same railroad dispatches a pair of dual-service DL-109 diesels out of Cedar Hill yard with a symbol to Boston. The train swings on to the main at Shoreline Jct. (BALL, DONAHUE)

When it came to classic electrics, in my book, the New Haven had them all, sans GG-1. And when it came to the crew's affections toward their locomotives, I doubt if any railroad could top the spirit and pride of New Haven's electric crews. A splashy "jet," a regal "flat bottom," and a beautiful "yellow jacket" appear on these pages, in case you didn't know. Technically, we're speaking of the EP-5 rectifier whining through Hell Gate's span with the eastbound *Senator;* a box cab EP-3 westbound under the bow arches at Glenbrook, Conn., and a streamlined EF-2 on a symbol, as viewed from Hell Gate's "rainbow." (BALL)

To this day, there is a constant parade of electric M.U. (Multiple Unit) trains in and out of New York City—almost enough to keep the rails warm! These three scenes are from the 50's, but for all practical purposes (overlooking the paint), these scenes might have been taken in the 1920's since M.U. equipment changed very little over the next forty years. Above, a New York Central local from White Plains, N.Y., clicks along through snow near Scarsdale, loaded with the *Herald Tribune*, the *Times*, and commuters! At the upper right, an owl-eyed Pennsy New Brunswick express barrels down the Jersey main, while below, New Haven "muts" notch out of Port Chester, N.Y., with a New York to Stamford, Conn., local. (BALL)

Some more variations in the New York metropolitan area railroad scene. During a mid-day lull, four New Haven "washboards" cross over from the Stamford, Conn. passenger yard over main's 4, 2, 1 and on to 3 for the run into New York City. The view is from SS-38 tower. To the right a squat (to say the least!) Pennsy class B-1 "Keystone" switcher works last trick in the vast Sunnyside yards in Long Island City. Farther out on the Island (opposite), one of Long Island's nineteen H-10's works an eastbound freight through Mineola—clear stack, crisp weather, blue sky. (BALL, SHAUGHNESSY, LINK)

One might tersely state that electric locomotives are nothing more than small motors hidden between small- or medium-size driving wheels, with a metal housing covering the motors and some electrical switchgear—and of course room for engineer and fireman—an organization for all the world like a box car! Well, on these pages are some *very different* electrics.

At the left, a 600 volt d.c. New York Central P-motor rumbles out of the long Park Avenue tunnel from Grand Central Station. This pin-striped beauty is heading the stainless steel *Ohio State Limited* out to Harmon, where diesels will take over. At right, some split-second 11,000 volt action on the Pennsy at Elizabeth with three fast-moving trains. The motor is one of two Westinghouse class E-3b rectifiers on B-B-B trucks. Below, *the classic locomotive:* maroon and gold GG-1 #4864 rustles the leaves hurrying out of Philadelphia with a New York-bound clocker. (HARWOOD, BALL, BALL)

One of the greatest places around New York to watch steam was Harmon. Engines would be dispatched from the ready track and would loop over the mainline (on "the ladder") and back down into the station to take over from the electric locomotives. Once the highball was given, the locomotive would blast under the waiting room, under the service road, and out into the open. A mighty Niagara gets out of Harmon with train #43, the *Knickerbocker*, in May 1953. In February of the same year, a Hudson moves a Buffalo express out of Harmon, where by late summer steam would be but a memory. (HARWOOD, BALL)

The Hudson and Mohawk valleys—historic, legendary, romantic—where Commodore Vanderbilt forged the New York to Buffalo railroad system that was completed in 1867. Three 1950 scenes from the New York Central show zebra-striped E-7's heading the *Ohio State Limited* westward out of Harmon; a Niagara bounding down the Mohawk Valley with the New York-bound *Missourian;* and a classic Hudson-type along the Hudson River opposite Bear Mountain (NOWAK)

The anthracite roads, whose revenues were once all in the coal-bonanza, were, oddly, among the first regional roads to go wholesale diesel. As if having nothing to do with coal, their diesels were flamboyantly colorful. At left, two new FM trainmasters power a Scranton-bound hotshot through the Delaware Water Gap in September 1953. Below, in the same year, one of New York, Ontario & Western's FT quartets gets under way out of Middletown, N.Y. with symbol BC-3 for Scranton. On this page, Lackawanna's train No. 6, the *Lackawanna Limited*, accelerates east out of the Gap, en route to Hoboken, while below, an A-B-B-A set of Lehigh & New England FA's crosses the Delaware River from Portland, Pa., into Columbia, N.J., with the Penn Argyll to Maybrook turn. (BALL, MALINOSKI, DONAHUE, MALINOSKI)

Folk legend in diesel dress. Lackawanna's mythical princess, *Phoebe Snow*, is caught under the wires at Millburn, N.J., on her westward dash to Buffalo. At right, Reading's home-built T-1 #2120 pulls out of Pottsville with empties for the nearby mines. The engineer is profiled in the cab, hand upon the throttle. Opposite, one of CNJ's classic Pacifics of *Blue Comet* fame charges east out of Bound Brook, N.J., under billowing steam. (WOOD, BALL, FOGG)

The Pennsylvania Railroad's striking thoroughbred, the storied K-4 Pacific, was perfected and built in 1914. For three decades thereafter, the K-4's moved the *Broadway*, the *Trail Blazer*, the *Liberty Limited*, the *Admiral*, the *Spirit of St. Louis*—all of Pennsy's varnish—until the arrival of the T-1 steam duplex and the diesels. The K-4 was *the archetype* of Pennsy motive power, and unlike most famous steam locomotives, it survived and outlasted many a diesel! People who missed the grand era of steam passenger railroading had a second chance along the New Jersey shore where the K-4's preserved a stronghold up through the mid-50's. In a scene reminiscent of the war years, the 5351 and the 3750 approach South Amboy at ballast scorching speed in January 1957. At right, the 3807 prepares for a dash along the shore, gathering momentum out of South Amboy, under a calling card of steam. (WOOD, BALL)

It would be hard to say which last-of-steam safari meant the most to me. Certainly no steam show could have topped Pennsy's "great middle division M-1 parade" in 1955. Westbound M-1 #6979 strides past with empties while sister 6717's headlight comes into view from that direction. Below left, the late Bud Rothaar caught the 6724 at Mifflin, Pa., just as the engineer opened her wide. Below, Don Wood froze the dramatic passage of 6758 pounding through Duncannon, coal dust flying! (BALL, ROTHAAR, WOOD)

A look at Pennsy after dark. Jim Shaughnessy's special pleasure was to walk into a railroad yard after dark and capture on film the wonderment of behind-the-scenes railroading—the dark shadows, the highlighted contours of the great locomotives, the atmosphere of mystery. A marvelous subject was, of course, the locomotives of Pennsy—grimy and hot. Three studies find I-1 #4523 riding the Elmira, N.Y., table; I-1's #4587 and L-1's #1682 passing in the night at Elmira; and a beautiful after-dark portrait of L-1's #110 at Hagerstown, Md. (SHAUGHNESSY)

My most vivid impressions of Pennsy are plain-to-the-point-of-being-ugly, ill-maintained steam locomotives, working for and aft, on long trains of tuscan hoppers. To a PRR fan, these scenes are no doubt beautiful; to me, they are memories—fond memories —of the very end of steam locomotion on the *Standard Railroad of the World.* At the upper left, an I-1 and two diesels struggle along on a Northumberland to Mt. Carmel ore train, near Orphanage, Pa. Below left, a rare treat in May 1954, "up on the curve" as a J-1 puts in an appearance drifting into Horseshoe with empty hoppers. Above, east of Shamokin, two "Hippos" do what comes naturally to them—shove on the rear of a heavy train. On the head end two more ranting I-1's. (MALINOSKI, BALL, BALL)

Evening tranquility in Cloverdale, Va., is interrupted by the flagstop arrival of N&W's train No. 2 from Cincinnati. At night in this sleepy mountain land, a passing train is like music heard in a restless sleep. Above, a more workaday scene as Western Maryland's big 4-8-4 #1404 hammers north against a cross wind near Lurgan, Pa. Fanciers of steam generally rate the WM 1400's as perhaps the ugliest Northerns ever built. On the other hand, the big, rawboned 4-8-4's impressed me with their no-nonsense look of utility, not to mention their immaculate maintenance and beautiful paint. The vestibule-cab engine was turned out by Baldwin in 1947, well after road diesels were in service on the Western Maryland. This raw February 1954 scene is from #1404's last days of regular operation. (LINK, BALL)

As late as 1956, coal-conscious Norfolk & Western was turning out virtually new, completely rebuilt locomotives in its Roanoke shops. To the left is an example: a 1918-built K-2 class Mountain, streamlined in 1945, riding the Shaeffer's Crossing table after coming in off her run by way of the wash rack. Three days earlier, I had watched this locomotive emerge from the paint shed, a glistening beauty cloaked in gloss black, tuscan, and gold! On this page, a scene typical of railroading's 24-hour operations, as well as "Norfolk & Western country." The town cop and the cook arriving at Burn's Restaurant seem unaware of the noisy intrusion by N&W's Y-6 and first 51 through downtown Stanley, Va. Moments earlier the door slamming on that Chevy would have echoed up and down the street! (BALL, LINK)

In 1881, Frederick J. Kimball, vice president of the newly formed Norfolk & Western, "discovered" bituminous coal; he found a local blacksmith was successfully burning it in a forge. In 1883, the N&W shipped the first carload of bituminous and has ever since been solidly in the black-diamond business. N&W thenceforth consisted mainly of huge, long, black coal trains and of necessity employed the most powerful locomotives to move them.

Blue Ridge, the Sherman Hill of the East, provided some of the greatest shows in steam railroading. The pillars stand tall as the great engines battle upgrade. The noise is deafening as an A and a Y-6 lead the parade. On the rear end, the coal-fired turbine Jawn Henry, along with another Y-6, assures an overwhelming 562,460 lbs. of tractive effort to move the huge train. In the photograph opposite, the brakeman has pulled the pin on panting pusher #2179 just after cresting Blue Ridge. The Y-6 compound pops off, while drifting to a halt. She'll return down the hill to a siding east of Vinton to wait for her next assignment back up the hill. (HARWOOD, YOUNG)

This is a land where the school and grocery store are "just over the hill"—perhaps five miles away by road, a half mile walking through the railroad tunnel. A land where mine shafts and dwellings are nestled against hillsides. Where men work beneath, in the silent dark world of shallow coal. In this bleak land, Norfolk & Western moves the black bounty. These four photographs show N&W as I knew it.

At upper left, a ponderous, elephantine Y-6 lays over in Yeager. Below is a quick from-the-car glimpse of another Y-6 shoving hard to keep a coal train moving through the Blue Ridge.

On this page (right), a chunky S-1 switcher throws 65,000 lbs. of tractive effort into the job of classifying cars in Williamson. Above, a photograph taken from the car window along the Tug fork of a Y-6 as she pours it on, rolling a coal train west out of Williamson. The sound is deafening! (BALL)

I try to refrain from who-built-the-best-and-why arguments about steam locomotives. Naturally, I have favorites, although I'll admit to appreciating performance records of not-so-favorite locomotives. Any way you look at it, top honors should go to Norfolk & Western's impressive A-class 2-6-6-4, a greyhound-articulated capable both of racing 14,500 tons on level ground and dragging heavy tonnage up mountains. One of these long-legged beauties, the 1213, swings her boiler out on a tight curve, pounding hellbent through a drizzle with eastbound empties out of Portsmouth, Ohio.

On this page, two scenes of a pastoral Norfolk & Western. Above, a J-class 4-8-4 #609 handles the eastbound *Pocahontas* through the beautiful apple-orchard country near Christiansburg, Va., while at right, un-streamlined K-2 #105 approaches the outskirts of Bristol, Va., whistling for the many rural grade crossings. Although not often photographed, the unshrouded K's remained in local freight service between Bristol and Radford well into 1958. (BALL, MALINOSKI, COLLECTION)

Just looking at a map of the Virginian will give you an idea of the road's function. On the west end, "fingers of branchlines" reach into the rich bituminous mines in West Virginia; then, from nearby Elmore, it's a straight shot all the way to Sewalls Point, Va. on the tidewater. On this spread, I've tried to include the many personalities of the VGN. At upper left, train No. 4, a three-car accommodation, crosses Gooney Otter Creek trestle behind a PA class 4-6-2. At bottom left, a huge 6,800 h.p. GE electric lays over at Roanoke, while above right, two black and yellow GE rectifiers are tied down for the night at Roanoke. At the immediate right, one of the company's huge super-power Lima 2-6-6-6's mothers 15,000 tons of coal from Roanoke toward the tidewater. In a sense, Virginian had it all. (COLLECTION, BALL, SHAUGHNESSY, COLLECTION)

The Great Smokies—inaccessible country where the past seems still present and where railroading is difficult and dangerous. Left, two Southern Railway F-3's rumble around a sharp bend, flanges squealing, on the line from Old Fort to Ridgecrest, N.C., with a freight from Asheville. Below, tucked deep within the mountains, are four FT's near Hot Springs, N.C., on the Asheville line, en route to Memphis. At right, Central of Georgia's smart *Nancy Hanks II* arrives in Atlanta, after a 293-mile trip from Savannah. (DONAHUE, DONAHUE, LAVAKE)

The beautiful Berkshire. Sired by the same design team that specified *governors, statesmen,* and *generals* for its 4-8-4's, the Richmond, Fredericksburg & Potomac's freight counterparts were equally handsome. RF&P's 2-8-4 #577 is seen in 1950 at Potomac yards, Va., alongside C&O 2-10-2 #2955. At right, one of Florida East Coast's tasteful red, yellow, black, and silver E-6's waits to head the *Dixie Flagler* and its roster of affluent patrons north out of Miami. At the far right, a far cry from Flagler's diesel-powered showcase, Seaboard's Jacksonville switcher works the yard in May 1950, a few days before her retirement. (RONFOR, WOLFE, LA VAKE)

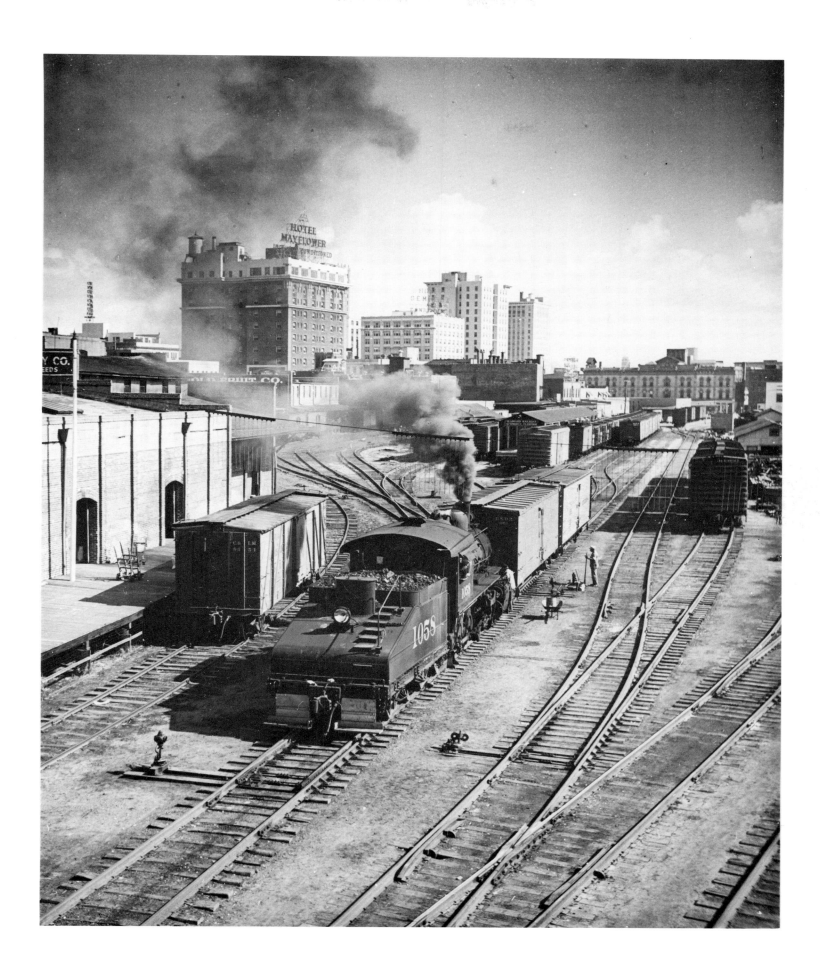

During the waning years of steam, a few rail-photographers courted the growlers. Although the first diesels were indeed colorful, steam had the color of railroading. I doubt if any of the pictures on this spread would have provoked intense excitement at the time they were taken. They are now included simply because even these trains and locomotives are as far removed from the railroad scene as the steam locomotive. The low-nosed hood units of today bear little if any resemblance to these first-generation diesels.

At the upper left, Southern's *Tennessean* makes its 7:40 p.m. departure out of Memphis behind Alco DL-109 power. The diesels will forward the streamliner to Bristol, Tenn., where Norfolk and Western steam will take over as far as Monroe. Below left, beautifully painted Central of Georgia F-3's #902 and #904 get southbound tonnage on the move out of Smarr, Georgia. Above, the die is cast on L&N's great 2-8-4's as F-7's take over nearly all the coal assignments for The Old Reliable. On August 8, 1956, when these two "black cats" departed DeCoursey, only one 2-8-4 was chalked up on the board, the #1973, crew called for 6:01 p.m. (COLLECTION, COLLECTION, BALL)

Chesapeake & Ohio, a railroad whose profile—and mechanical department's philosophy—required no fewer than twenty popular wheel arrangements, offered train-watchers a contrast of power as varied as the land it served. Above, a pipe-laden K-3 Mike approaches JC interlocking at Clifton Forge, Va., while at right, one of the road's huge 2-6-6-6 Alleghenies is serviced at Thurmond, W.Va. At the far right, a K-4 Kanawha scorches the ballast out of Catlettsburg, Ky., highballing the merchandise. (DONAHUE, HASTINGS, BALL)

In 1803, The National Road—or the first part of it, called the Cumberland Road—was completed for wagon trains from the Potomac River to the Ohio River at Wheeling. In 1827, plans to lay track over this route were worked out and the Baltimore & Ohio Railroad was chartered. Wheeling soon became its western hub.

In the mid-1950's, Wheeling, with its old flat-roofed buildings crowded between hill and river, offered a haven for steam power. The center of B&O's activity on the West Virginia side was Benwood Jct., where five lines radiated out; one of them crossed the broad Ohio River and immediately encountered mountains for most of the 41 miles over to Holloway, Ohio, affording onlookers some of the heaviest railroad action in the last years of steam. The shots on these two pages were made by J. J. Young, a native of Wheeling and one of the best railroad photographers in America. Above, in weather typical of Wheeling, two Mikes get out of town in a turn-of-the-century setting. Across the page, big EM-1 articulated #651 steams past SW tower on a Holloway turn, all in all, the perfect portrait of the twin-stacked majesty of this most beautiful of articulateds. (YOUNG)

On this page, coal comes into Wheeling behind huge EM-1 #676, which is also pushing two dead ex-NYO&W FT's that broke down on the run over from Grafton. The neat row of frame houses lined up along the tracks is seen everywhere throughout railroad West Virginia. Across the page, a nocturnal scene in Benwood Jct. as the hogger oils around L-2 #1697, while the ashcat fills the tank, and a sister 0-8-0 shuffles cars in the yard. Below, an unlikely Mutt-and-Jeff combination works westbound tonnage under March skies near Bellaire, Ohio. (YOUNG)

Contrasts. A quartet of F-7's, glistening from the rain, enters the interlocking at McKenzie Tower, west of Cumberland. The tracks in the foreground lead up the Patterson Creek cut-off, bypassing Cumberland. The tracks in front of #182 lead toward Keyser, where a steamer will lock couplers with the diesels for the grueling climb up Seventeen Mile grade. On the right, an EM-1 etches black smoke into the gloomy skies as she departs Benwood Jct. for Holloway. (DONAHUE, YOUNG)

Good locomotive design and its satisfying appeal can withstand the critical test of time. In 1946, Miss Olive Dennis, a civil engineer with the B&O, designed the streamlined dress that was applied to four 1927 P-7 class locomotives for the *Cincinnatian.* The result was, to me, the most satisfying streamlining of any steam locomotive. During their twilight, many of us waited out in the midwestern countryside to pay last respects to the great Cincinnatian ladies. The 5303 is nearing the end of her career on this lovely April evening in 1956. The location is Lima, Ohio. At right, in the summer of '56, massive 2-8-8-4 #7605 rolls grandly down the iron with empties from the lake port at Lorain. (STIRTON, BALL)

In the East, I was obsessed with the B&O's great stable of steam. If the last few pages have not adequately justified my obsession, then perhaps the shots on these two pages will do it. Above, an ex-Boston & Maine 4-8-2, rebuilt by the B&O, lets the world know she's leaving town, departing Willard, Ohio, in 1957. A few miles west, on the flat tangent rail, the 73″ drivered machine will be in full stride. Across the page, Q-4 class 2-8-2 #467 makes a smoky appearance at the Jaite, Ohio, order station with tonnage southbound from Cleveland to Akron. It's a bleak February day in 1957, and in a matter of days, steam will be gone from this line, leaving it forever quiet. (HARWOOD)

GANGBUSTERS! The crossing lights flash, a whistle sounds, and in a second, three million pounds of EM-1's storm into town! In September 1956, three EM-1's worked northbound coal on the Lake branch, through and out of W. Farmington, Ohio, in a show of steam-powered fury never to be repeated on the B&O. The participants in this grand event were the 7625, 7603, and 7611. (HARWOOD)

In the summers of '55 and '56, my train chasing was confined largely to the state of Ohio, and in particular, the ore/coal lines that were used as conveyor belts between the Great Lakes and the coal fields. Each summer, when the Great Lakes opened to navigation, the single track iron of the Pennsylvania between Columbus and Sandusky would come alive with 10,000-ton trains. The brute power for the enormous trains was the huge J-1 class 2-10-4. On the following pages, we "chase" one of these coal trains along the line. Between slides, 16mm movies, and black and white, rarely did I stay with one camera for both the coming *and* going shots! At left, two of the massive power plants move up the passing track at Chatfield, Ohio. On this page, another tandem, the 6412 and the 6482, sets out bad-order cars at Carrothurs. The interlocking is the connecting line to Tyro and the main at Toledo Jct. (BALL, COLLECTION, COLLECTION)

Northbound #6488 passes #6402 and #6163 in the hole with a seemingly endless train of coal-laden hoppers. The lead crew enjoys the air and a chance to inspect the passing train.

On this page, the two demons from Hades put on a dramatic show, getting out of the passing track and on with their business. Witnessing such a spectacle, it didn't seem possible that steam railroading was coming to an end. (COLLECTION)

On the following pages, Nickel Plate's Berkshire #746 slips on frosty rails getting under way out of Vermilion, Ohio, after stopping for a board. Common in the railroad scene are the various maintenance-of-way shacks and shanties that themselves have a compelling attraction on any railroad journey. The time is Thanksgiving 1957, and the celebrated 2-8-4's still carry out the road-freight assignments. (BALL)

In the mid-50's, to me the glamour trains were the secondary trains, freight and passenger, that still drew steam. New York Central's No. 410, a nameless overnight mail-and-coach affair, was such a train. Opposite, Mohawk #3049, popping off into the frosty air, rattles the interlocking at Valley Jct., 17 miles from its Cincinnati destination on No. 410. Mike #1959 waits in the clear. On this page, Nickel Plate's Ft. Wayne local with Hudson #173 waits in the clear at Mentone, Indiana, for train No. 8 to run by. After traffic subsides, #173 gets her orders and heads east. By now the drizzle has turned into a soaking rain. (WITTENBORN, BALL, BALL)

Framed in nature's own setting, three New York Central F-7 A-units leave the Pennsy main at Brady Lake, Ohio, and follow the old LE&P toward Cleveland. At right, one of New York Central's distinctive Mohawks—an L-3a—steams through the yard leads in Cincinnati. In this 1955 view it is evident from the black wash that Central did some maintenance on steam right up to the end. On the right-hand page, a close-up look at one of Central's chisel-nosed Baldwin sharks. (HARWOOD, BALL, BALL)

On this page, a farewell to New York Central steam—forever. A black-washed H-7e Mikado and two F-7's line up at the Riverside yards in Cincinnati for that one final moment. After the proud portrait is committed to film, 1977 will make her last run, to the scrap track 3,000 feet back, to have her fire dropped for the last time. (MARSH STUDIOS)

English writer C. Hamilton Ellis once wrote that "the grandeur of steam locomotion is such that little comment is needed."

In the peerage of the last steam-powered limiteds, one train carried on in the grand manner after diesels had taken over virtually everywhere. That train, of course, was New York Central's *James Whitcomb Riley.* It's impossible not to comment on Harry Stirton's moving portrait of Hudson #5409 sweeping around the curve at Lafayette, Indiana, with the *Riley* on her tail. I believe all the ingredients are present to make this *the picture* of railroading in its golden years.

Above, in a Christmas-card setting, New York Central's 2-8-2 #1576 breaks the winter silence, heading a local freight through the wooded hills of southern Indiana. Both photographs were made in 1956. (STIRTON, BALL)

The world is white; the wind has an edge like a wet knife. The snow swirls and swirls and comes down thick from the grey sky. An old-fashioned blizzard hits Indiana, and the railroads gird for battle. On the left page, a Monon A-B-A set of F-3's pulls into Green-castle to wait for the northbound *Thor-oughbred* to run around. The crew will have a chance to warm up beside the pot-bellied stove and sample some of the operator's fresh hot brew. On this page, an Illinois Central 4-8-2 runs through lingering snow flurries, hurrying southbound freight through Richmond, Illinois. Below, IC 2-8-2 #1537 steams north under a low winter sun near Aldridge, Illinois. All three scenes were shot in January '57, '58, and '59. (BALL, MEYER, MEYER)

Throughout the age of steam, cults of locomotive worshipers have extolled the merits of one railroad's steam power over another's, on the basis of either looks or operating statistics. Mistakenly, Illinois Central's steam power was rarely praised in either category. In the first of these studies (left) of Illinois Central power in action, I defy anyone to fault the beautiful lines of Mountain-type #2524 backing through the Paducah, Ky., yard to pick up her tonnage. Above, the 1537 charges northward across a spindly trestle near Ware, Illinois. On this page, Central-type 2-10-2 #2739 uses her incredible 118,000 lbs. tractive effort to get a coal train out of Paducah. This was the IC in 1959! (MEYER, BALL, BALL)

During the days of steam on the Wabash, the crews took pride in running their trains as fast as locomotive and rail conditions would permit. "To Wabash" became a verb in railroad jargon meaning to run like hell, and likewise, a "Wabash artist" was a fast-running engineer. Steam is gone from the Wabash, but the crew on this Alco diesel-powered freight has not forgotten how "to Wabash." The trio of engines is out-pacing a vicious squall-line near West Lebanon, Indiana. (BALL)

To the left, Chicago & Eastern Illinois' blue and orange train No. 18, *The Humming Bird*, makes a good 80 mph through the flat Indiana countryside near Clinton. Below, a queen enters Chicago as Santa Fe's Alco PA #72 and her B-unit mate bring the *Texas Chief* into town. (COLLECTION)

The engineer of Rock Island's *Des Moines Rocket* backs his train out of La Salle Street Station after discharging passengers. These tracks are also used by the New York Central and Nickel Plate. (COLLECTION)

Chicago, Chicago...! The Roosevelt Road overpass has always been *the* location for shooting the great variety of trains in Chicago. At left, Wabash's *Banner Blue* pulls into Dearborn Station at 5:40 p.m. past a Chicago & Western Indiana switcher. The waiting Santa Fe *El Capitan* will depart in five minutes. Below, Alco PA diesels head out of Union Station with Pennsy's *Pennsylvania Limited* at 6:00 p.m. (BALL, COLLECTION)

Nose to nose. The *Columbian* arrives in Chicago six minutes off the advertised and passes an outbound *80-minute train* to Milwaukee. To the left of the Canal Street tower is the huge Merchandise Mart; to the right, a North Shore express to Milwaukee crosses the Chicago River on the CTA tracks. Above right, an F-3a Pacific takes over 5th and Clybourn streets, departing Milwaukee with the *Chippewa.* To its right, DL-109 #14 waits for departure time with the *Afternoon Hiawatha.* Below right, home-built diesel #5901 departs Great Falls, Montana, with the modest accommodations of train No. 118 for Harlowton. (COLLECTION)

Minnesota is known for Paul Bunyan, the legendary giant who accomplished enormous tasks. On the following pages, two Paul Bunyan-sized locomotives arrive and depart Proctor, Minnesota, on the Duluth Missabe & Iron Range. On the left, a Yellowstone 2-8-8-4; on the right, a Union type 2-10-0. (SHAUGHNESSY, KING)

Granger grandeur. To Carl Sandburg, "the milk of its wheat, the red of its clover." To railroaders, the Burlington railroad. The hallmark of the Q, of course, is fluted stainless steel *Zephyr* steamliners. On this page, the sleek *Twin Cities Zephyr* skirts South St. Paul (left), while below, an E-7 and the shovel-nosed "Silver Knight" accelerate an extra mail train west through Downers Grove, Illinois.

Across the page, one of Burlington's magnificent 0-5 class 4-8-4's hammers along west of Plano, Illinois, under a haze of coal smoke. Time and again during the grain and sugar beet harvests in the mid-50's, the road pressed some of its stored 0-5's into service. Enginemen were not surprised to find that the big engines could still outrun the freight diesels that replaced them. (BALL, BALL, BUHRMASTER)

During "my decade"—or for that matter, any time from the turn of the century through 1960—no railroad terminal could compare with the color of St. Louis Union Station, when it came to the great variety of railroads and name trains that assembled under the huge train shed. Here is a sampling of color once offered to the St. Louis train watcher on no fewer than 52 stub tracks and on no fewer than 15 different railroads: from Pennsy Tuscan and gold PA's for the *Admiral* to a lone "bluebird" Nickel Plate PA for No. 6 to Cleveland; from Missouri Pacific's impressive 4-8-2 on the *Sunflower* to Frisco's smart red, yellow, grey, and silver *Texas Special*. (COLLECTION)

In my youth, I spent many an hour with my Uncle Willy Hill, then roundhouse foreman for the Missouri Pacific at Osawatomie, Kansas. I vividly recall walking, as we always did, around the great 4-8-4's and 4-8-2's, 2-10-2's and 2-8-2's. I can remember going around back to look at the new diesels. They were a novelty and the colors were pretty. As long as steam was around, the diesels "out back" didn't make much difference. In 1954, years later, I went after the last 2200's on the MP with my camera, but I was too late. Slides of shiny Alco and GM diesels is what I got. Friend and Missouri Pacific-devotee Joe Collias recorded the splendid goings of 4-8-4 #2201 on the Illinois Division at Bixby in January 1954 (above). At the upper right, one of the company's admittedly smart *Eagle* diesels gets a bath. Below it, three Baldwin "baby-face" diesels have a good roll on a westbound stock train, near Sandy Hook, Mo. (COLLIAS, MP, COLLECTION)

Kansas City was always the best railroad town for me. On many weekends, I'd ride UP into K.C., walk miles of tracks, and prowl around the engine terminals to get a close look at the objects of my affection. At left is a look at super power at rest, #905 being a Kansas City Southern Lima-built 2-10-4 with a staybolted boiler, rated at 310 lbs., and riding on 70″ drivers. Super power! On this page, the personalities of three railroads are very apparent in the view inside Kansas City Terminal Railway's roundhouse. All three locomotives are Pacifics, but all are remarkably individual, reflecting the basic philosophies of their owners. In the foreground, the tidy, well-tailored look of Katy; the comfortable, homely look of Burlington in its #6608; and in the rear, the lordly look of Missouri Pacific. (With diesels, I don't believe there are enough paint hues in the world to produce anything approaching the honest, individualistic personalities the steamers possess.) (SMITH)

A Rock Island 0-8-0 clanks into sight and past, going about its routine chores around the vast Kansas City yards. No smoke, whistles, or waves, not even a train, merely this engine going past—a sight that conveys most of what railroading is all about. (COLLECTION)

The trains of Lawrence! At the upper left, Rock Island's big 4-8-4 #5103 has taken on water in Lawrence and two miles west of town is still struggling to get the tonnage moving. The little Midland schoolhouse still stands today, though most rural schoolhouses have gone the way of steam. Several miles east of Lawrence, in Muncie, Kansas, a single DL-109 hurries the westbound *Texas Rocket*. On this page, Santa Fe's only attempt at steam streamlining—the 84″ drivered Hudson #3460—sweeps into Lawrence with the eastbound *Antelope*. The #3460, or "Blue Goose," was a regular visitor to Lawrence until Santa Fe gave up passenger steam in 1953. (OLMSTED, MALINOSKI, OLMSTED)

These photographs are documents of what was once part of my everyday life in Lawrence. I took mostly slides and movies, while Bob Olmsted took black and white. I am grateful he was around! Here are three moods of Lawrence. At the upper left, train No. 40, *The Kansan*, leaves town behind a loud 4-8-2 and passes a 4-12-2 on a westbound extra. At left, while the town sleeps, Union Pacific's train No. 37, the *Pony Express*, makes its 12:30 a.m. stop in Lawrence on its westward trek. Above, one of Santa Fe's huge 4-6-4's, the 3461, accelerates rapidly out of Lawrence toward Kansas City in a nocturnal scene of smoke, steam, and approaching dawn. The train is No. 28, *The Antlope*. (OLMSTED)

Union Pacific Kansas Division! Magic in the days of steam! Standard power across the Osage Plains of eastern Kansas was the 4-12-2, 4-6-2, and earlier series 4-8-4. Not pictured are the ubiquitous 2-8-2 and 2-10-2. At the upper left, my personal favorite, a 4-12-2, the engine that held sway on most of the big freights on the Kansas Division, here holding down the iron just west of Topeka, near the junction of the Denver and Grand Island mains. Below, freshly shopped Pacific #2910 streaks west out of Topeka with the K.C.-Ellis local; above, a few years later, the same train leaves Lawrence in a backlit setting. The location is about 1,000 feet west of the station—perhaps the best trackside view in Lawrence. The year is 1953. (BALL, SMITH, OLMSTED)

131

Most UP regular trains on the Kansas Division carried train numbers. I could always depend on No. 359 to run in at least four (or five) sections with a 9000 assigned. On the left, the first section of 359 is shown three miles east of Lawrence, rolling west with the high cars. On this page, the 9505 hammers into the curve at Midland, two miles west of Lawrence with an extra that will run up through Marysville, Kansas, and onto the Nebraska Division at Gibbon. Below, the crew on the 9079 decided to take on water at Lawrence, rather than Topeka. With the 5000 class 2-10-2, a water stop in Lawrence was necessary, but with the larger tanked 4-12-2's, the SOP was to go on by and take on water at Topeka. Either way, these great locomotives provided plenty of entertainment! (KERRIGAN, BALL, BALL)

"Short-grass country," the country of "prairie wool," where stock can be fattened as fast as grain-fed stock; where barbed wire runs for hundreds of miles; where the wind is ever present; and where Colorado & Southern conducts its business of railroading. On this page, venerable C&S 2-10-2 #902 works freight over the lonely Colorado uplands toward such only-in-America places as Lone Tree, Horse Creek, and Chugwater. At right, the 900 works freight across the endless miles of northern Colorado on a giant stage under the wide western sky. In 1957 when these pictures were taken, steam, and only steam, moved the freight along the C&S. (COLLINS, BALL)

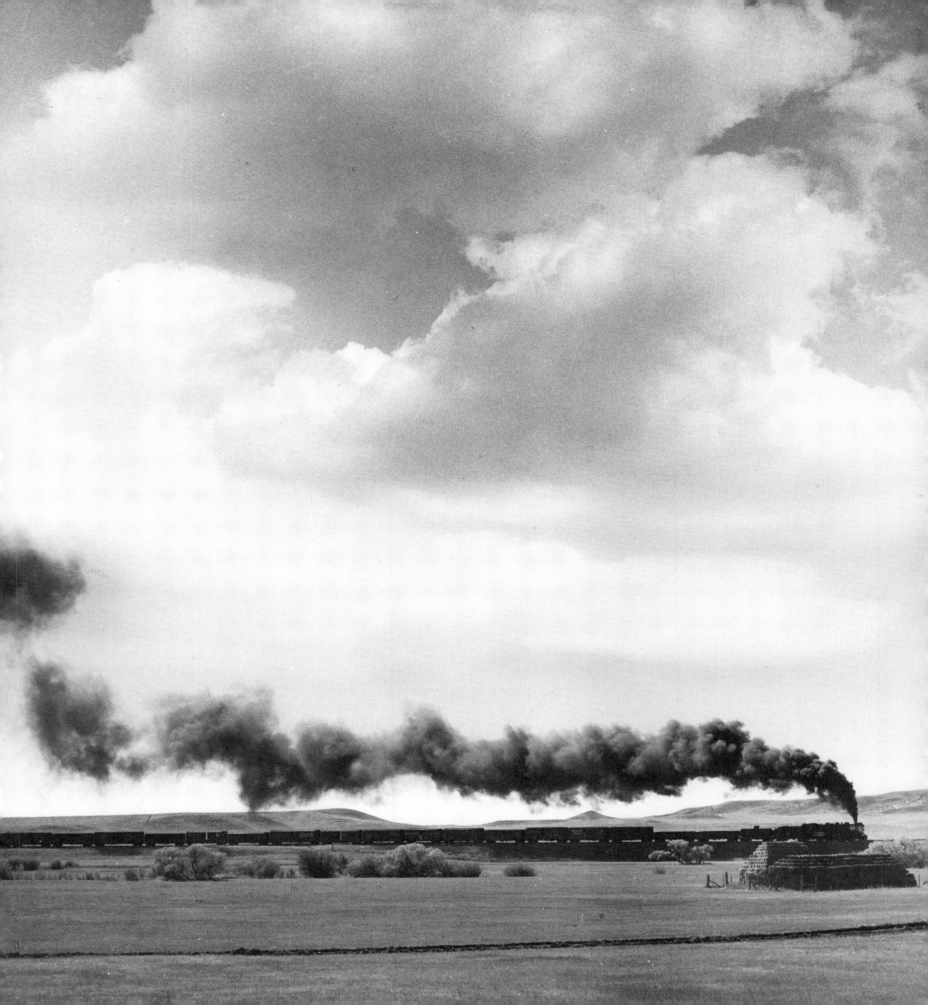

In the Ruby Canyon along the Colorado River, the scenery is awesome, with colorful rock formations, cliffs, and canyons of pink-red rocks. It is still an empty, unsettled land, with large portions untouched since the Donner party in 1846. A typical rock formation provides the background for the lead unit of an FT-powered Rio Grande freight en route from Denver to Salt Lake City.

The story repeated. In 1940, EMD's barnstorming FT demonstrator #103 walked tonnage unassisted up Rio Grande's 2 percent Soldier Summit in Utah's Wasatch Plateau. The diesel era was dramatically introduced. A decade and a half later (at right), the story is repeated again, only this time with newer GP-7's and no steam to contend with. (HALE)

The narrow-gauge empire, something I have neglected from the standpoints of both history and rail photography. The diminutive 3-foot gauge scared me away—too small to be of interest. How wrong I was! At left, the very essence and flavor of big-time railroading is present as the locomotives are serviced at Chama, N.M. Below, K-36 Mike #483 battles west of Laboto Trestle with a stock extra, while at right and just as on a standard-gauge railroad, a pusher shoves hard on the rear, near "Jukes Tree" on the run to Chama. A microcosm of the mainline carriers. (HALE, HAND, HAND)

Out of Cheyenne and far across the western horizons, where once trod the Silurian steam behemoths of the Union Pacific, only Big Boy, the world's largest steam locomotive, survived into the late 50's. After diesels had replaced virtually everything else in steam on the UP, Big Boy continued to make a stand, seemingly in outright challenge to the diesels. Big Boy, the quintessence of steam's final development—indeed the very *symbol* of steam's survival—is shown on these pages in its twilight.

Above left, the low western sun sets on the busy Cheyenne engine terminal as #4003 is being prepared to go out and do battle with Sherman Hill. To the left, and still huge under Wyoming's endless sky, Big Boy #4020 makes easy work of its short train, racing off the Dale cutoff. Above, Big Boy heads into the sunset—both literally and figuratively. (BALL, BALL, HALE)

Union Pacific. The name ... the railroad: pioneer transportation that conquered the West, always having the biggest and most powerful locomotives to insure that it remained conquered. The story of UP's insatiable thirst for horsepower is partially told, in transition, at daybreak in Rawlins, Wyoming (above), as a 16-wheeled gas turbine gets a fruit block underway past a huge 4-6-6-4 Challenger. At the upper right, No. 6 waits for its highball out of Salt Lake City, while below, at Ogden, Challenger #3981 clumps off the turntable under the watchful eye of heavy Pacific #2219. (MALINOSKI, SIMS, STEINHEIMER)

"The perfect train picture." Ask the average rail-photographer what is required to come up with the perfect picture and he'll probably say a ¾ camera-to-train angle, tangent track, low side lighting, no phone poles or trees behind, and of course, smoke. The head-end crew on Great Northern's 2-10-2 #2186 went further to provide this "perfect picture"— throttle wide open, pops going full blast, roll- ing through near-zero temperature at Breck-enridge, Minn., in the summer of 1956. Facing page, Northern Pacific's flagship train, the *North Coast Limited,* heads through Jefferson River Canyon, between Bozeman and Butte, Montana. Behind the engines lies the Lewis & Clark Cavern. (COLLIAS, COL-LECTION)

On these two pages appears a hard-working mallet compound locomotive on the Northern Pacific, lugging what would have to be a very long train. If we could watch both trains (same locomotive on different runs) pass across the page, we'd count 7 cars on the left and 13 cars on the right! These are the rugged Idaho Bitterroots, where the ruling grade is a twisting and turning 4 percent; where it's "down on your knees" all the way up the awful Wallace Branch of the NP. Above, the 1920 Z-3 2-8-8-2 shakes heaven and earth —and the trestle at Dorsey. At right, an even more spectacular show fighting up the west slope of Lookout Pass Summit in 1953. (GRIFFITHS)

Out of one of two railroad tunnels within the city limits of Spokane emerges Union Pacific's train No. 67, en route to Wallace, Idaho. The locomotive is one of UP's heavy, Sweeny-stacked Pacifics. The same train will make the 130-mile return trip as No. 68. (GRIFFITHS)

Across the page, an A-B-B-A team of Alco freight diesels roars through the flat back country near Bend, Oregon, with a south-bound Spokane, Portland & Seattle hotshot. The line comes out of Portland, 257 miles away, and becomes the Oregon Trunk Railway between Wishram and Bend, a distance of 107 miles. The year is 1956. (BALL)

The Southern Pacific—a railroad whose far-flung dimensions are matched by its motive power; and a railroad whose operating department believed in letting its motive power roam the system, be it desert or mountain, 2-6-0 or 4-8-8-2.

A backdrop of towering Oregon firs, or snow-covered Cascades, would be more appropriate than the California desert for these studies of AC cab-forward power. At left, the "flip-flop boilered" 4228 beats along the tangent with a mile of general merchandise on her drawbar. Giving a formidable assist is a sister AC. A dead 2-8-2 goes along for the ride, destined for the Sacramento shops. In the view above, two of the monsters throw a screen of oil smoke into the California sky near Roseville in a scene somewhat reminiscent of a delicate Japanese silk print. (SWAN, SWAN, HALE)

In 1955, this was the new look on Southern Pacific helper districts. Three hoods—5605, 5606, and 5607—throb away on the rear of a Coast Division freight out of San Luis Obispo, midway between Los Angeles and San Francisco. On the right page, the beauti-ful *Daylight* leaves Los Angeles northbound in 1953 behind one of the glamorous GS-4 class Northerns. The colorful Lima engine was striped in a red, orange, black, and silver livery to match the train. (KELSO, KISTLER)

During "my decade," some of the most co-lorful diesels in America operated in and out of California. To the upper left, the *Los Angeles Limited* hits Cajon behind the screaming power of an FM Erie-built A-unit lashed up to Alco PB and PA units. Below left, the 19-car *San Joaquin Daylight* nears Mojave, Cal., in December 1953, filled with Christmas passengers. On this page, we've got a problem! Alco's off an earlier train ob-viously split the switch—ho-hum! While the situation is contemplated, F-7's pass by with a coal train. (SWAN, KISTLER, HALE)

Personal favorite. There is a popular notion that aesthetics must be sacrificed to brute power. Not so, when it came to Santa Fe and its huge 4-8-4. These locomotives were extraordinarily fine examples of the "perfect Baldwin mold." More important, they were creatures with the stamina to climb mountains and race across deserts.

Above, one of these great engines, the 2929, sweeps down Cajon on the last lap of its transcontinental journey into Los Angeles with the heavy *Grand Canyon Limited*. At right, sister 2923 assaults Cajon with the eastbound *Grand Canyon Limited*, her clean-fired blast crashing off the stone, her pops lifting high. (HALE)

Passengers aboard the *Grand Canyon Limited*
are witnesses to a mighty vision as the God of
High Iron pilots their train up Cajon Pass.
(HALE)

Santa Fe's only Fairbanks-Morse passenger diesels coil the gleaming *Super Chief* up through Cajon on the eastbound dash to Chicago. (HALE)

Two more closing scenes of Southern Pacific's most notable locomotives. Above, train No. 72, the "milk run" between San Francisco and Los Angeles, approaches San Luis Obispo behind a clean-fired Daylight 4-8-4; while to the right, the head brakeman waves from the cab of a northbound Coast Line freight; the Burbank Jct. operator hands up orders in this 1950 scene. (KELSO, STEIN-HEIMER)

By the end of my decade, the land was quiet;
an uneasy stillness that I knew would last,
never again to be broken by the thunder of
steam.

By year's end 1960, all mainline steam was memory in both the U.S. and Canada. I opened this chapter with Canadian steam; it's appropriate that I close it with Mexican steam, for south-of-the-border scenes such as these were to be seen for another decade.

Above, NdeM 2-8-0 #1562 rolls under a canopy of oil smoke on a southbound freight near Aguascalientes. Her beautiful lines betray her American C&NW heritage. At left, one of NdeM's modern boxpok-drivered 4-8-4's climbs through a downpour south of Quenetaro, her slow, even, clear exhaust reaching skyward. At right, as gutsy a show as one could ask for! FCM #203, a 2-8-0, and road engine NdeM #2100, a 2-8-2, blot out the heavens, handling an eastbound freight near Apizaco. The scene seems reminiscent of steam railroading on the Frisco. (HAND)

2

A CLOSER LOOK

AT&F

Recently, I had occasion to be on the *Broadway Limited* en route to Chicago. My roomette was a "Pacific series" Union Pacific 10 and 6, and our locomotive was an Amtrak-painted GG-1. Most of the train was made up of red, white ("silver mist"), and blue cars once foreign to Pennsy rails—hardly the picture one would conjure up if called upon to think about Pennsy and the *Broadway Limited.* Nevertheless, I was comfortable in my roomette and my thoughts had long returned to other times. The countryside rolled past my vessel of steel and I simply daydreamed my worries away as the rail joints clicked endlessly past. Soothing. As I watched, the fascination of the railroad quickly took hold and I was soon in a dreamy detachment, leaving any concept of time to the train crew. The catenary breezed by, mile after mile. Farms dotted the landscape now and then. Occasionally we'd flash through a growth of dense trees with rock cuts on either side. The phone wires dipped and raised, dipped and raised. For me, a long train ride provides that wonderful opportunity to relax, think, and simply gather thoughts, as the world rushes past.

Before long, we were slowing for Lancaster. The acute oily smell of composition brakeshoes was evident as we came to a quick stop in the old station. Back in the last car, off the end of the platform, we were still out in the country, next to the meadow grass and crickets. Following this lull in our steel parade, the signal was given and our big G headed out of the station towards the lingering red sun. We quickly crossed over onto the center track with a resounding clatter that imparted a feeling of urgency. From the vestibule door, I was treated to the racket of steel-on-steel—over crossovers and switches, under bridges and past buildings. At the edge of town, two boys on bikes waved from a bridge. We clattered past a switch engine and the crews exchanged "all's well" waves. Out in the country we began to really roll, sending cows and horses on the run. An elderly couple standing on their private crossing watched us flash by, and soon the green carpet of lush fields unrolled at an even faster pace. "Highballing," to a railroad man! When we'd overtake an automobile on the parallel road, its occupants would glance at us and wave as we passed. (Surely the wave must be an American institution!) Darkness was falling upon the gentle land, and "*Second call for dinner*" was being announced. After exchanging our GG-1 for three E-8's at Harrisburg, we were again under way. Up ahead, in the diner, one could not help feeling the warmth of fellow travelers—even the silent ones—all together in one cozy place. People make small talk and the waiters chuckle among themselves. Occasionally, laughter is heard back in the galley, and your hotel-on-wheels moves on into the night as the smell of good food fills the air. Families discuss the entrees on the menu and strangers talk to each other. The level of chatter and laughter increases as the train rolls on. Somewhere—in what seems to be the middle of nowhere—we encounter a red board, and the train is stopped. People turn to each other, kids press noses against the windows, and there is sudden interest in what's going on. A crew member passes through and mutters something about "TV-7 up ahead," and the steward tells one person there are "slow orders on the Middle Division." Whatever it is, the mystique of the railroad has taken hold; all conversation turns to trains and railroads. More often than not, the curious, compelling fascination of the railroad takes over and dominates its patrons (or, indeed, any who come in contact with it). We get our board, blow in the rear brakeman, and once again bore on into the night. Laughter and chatter fill the dining car. I have a nightcap, chat with the train crew, and head for bed.

Railroading doesn't have to begin with a locomotive—or for that matter, with a train. To some, railroading is twin ribbons of steel placed 4 feet 8-1/2 inches apart, anchored on wood crossties, ready to accommodate the nearest train. To others, railroading is waybills, tariffs, demurrage, per diem, and mileage allowance. Railroading can be the station, its people, tickets, and timetables. Or it can be the intricate maze of interlocking and dwarf signals at platform's end. Even a lonely signal, out on the edge of town, can convey all that is railroading. Everyone knows railroading is something that gets into your blood, once you've had a good dose of it (on this latter point, I wonder, for I've seen people become believers after their first encounter with a large steam locomotive).

Railroading is locomotives and trains and the other things too, but more important, it is the end product of an iron-and-steel network that built this nation. Railroading is at the same time a symbol of strength, a noisy romance, and a dying industry with country depots and line-side grain elevators. It is something that begins in a once-magnificent mid-city edifice (its platforms now vacant) and ends up out in the country somewhere. Yes, railroading is ACI and welded rail, CTC and electronic yards, tri-levels and Dash-2's. Railroading is *still* big, dominating, fascinating! And it will always be legend and ballad and folklore—all these things. But for anyone who includes "railroading" in his personal vocabulary, it is *his* kind of personal involvement with the railroad that is most important.

Alfred Holland Smith, president of the New York Central System from 1914 to 1924, boasted that his railroad was "95 per cent men and 5 per cent iron." The entire history of railroading is men—some of them well-known names—some from legend and ballad. Strong, tough industrialists like J.P. Morgan and William H. Vanderbilt—men who could build, or rip up, a thousand miles of track by the flick of a pen. Persistent innovators like Westinghouse, Janney, and Pullman, who made it their business to see that train travel was what it was meant to be—comfortable, clean, safe. And the Casey Joneses and the Jawn Henrys, the Lackawanna's Charles Haight and *Phoebe Snow;* Barrigers and Claytors—the list is endless! Someday I'll do a book on railroad people—from the telegraph office to the locomotive cab; the backshop and yard office, to the interlocking tower and general office. Railroading is a 24-hour business (without a roof) that would require volumes to portray. It's a business loaded with folk who never got over their childhood fascination with trains; a business in which seasoned railroaders can honest-to-goodness talk of their forefathers laying rail westward from the river bank, sweating through the passes and out across the wilderness—rights of way that, for the most part, exist today. Every railroad—across the board—has the same coal, steel, and sweat in its makeup. Each railroad is part of the land it built, and today serves.

The excitement of the rail adventure continues, but obviously it is changing. As a frankly sentimental, briefcase-carrying, London Fog wearing, dyed-in-the-Dacron commuter, I immediately think of Grand Central Terminal as an example of what has happened to much of the industry. In the early 1960's, I commuted into GCT on the New York Central. Certainly by that time the railroad industry—the nation's second largest—had reached a crisis (I might add that "crisis," according to Webster, means the turning point, the time of supreme trial or final choice, whereas today the word is often used to describe a moment when things begin to look bad), but the grand image of railroading was still very much in evidence. On many a morning, we'd be somewhere out of 125th Street Station when I'd look up from the paper and see the inbound *Century* on the parallel track. True, she had started to carry coaches, but the amenities of *le grand conveyance*—the cut flowers and white linen, porters and beige-uniformed dining-car personnel—were all there. Right next to us passed drawing rooms and staterooms, single and double bedrooms, a lounge car, the twin-unit diner, compartments with people ready to disembark—a beautiful blend of two-tone grey in the morning light. The "Hickory Creek" observation passed us, with its tail sign lit up in fluorescent blue. New York Central's prestigious *20th Century* had long been a household name—no doubt *the* most famous train in the world —and even in the early sixties this assessment was simply not questioned by the public. Indeed, the sixtieth anniversary of the *20th Century Limited* was celebrated on June 15, 1962, with a Diamond Jubilee Luncheon at the Biltmore. Our commuter train plunges into the dark of the long Park Avenue tunnel for the six-minute ride to Grand Central Terminal.

In the early 1960's, Grand Central was still beautiful. Every morning, this terminus was a hubbub of tens of thousands of commuters and long-distance travelers. Redcaps were everywhere. (Why, at one time, sixty-five redcaps were on hand for the *Century!*) High over the vast concourse, lights and gold leaf outlined the constellations of the heavens on the pale blue ceiling. Through the great south window, people constantly passed along the glass walkways in ever-changing patterns. In the center of both upper and lower levels, information booths handled lines of travelers inquiring about trains.

Alas, I use this great Beaux-Arts cathedral today and it has changed, reflecting what has happened to the railroad industry in general. No longer do *any* name trains depart from, or arrive in, Grand Central Terminal. No longer do red caps hustle down to meet and send off patrons. No longer does an army of mop men, squeegee men, and gum scrapers clean up every inch of GCT every night. The great windows are hazy with dirt, the gold leaf has flaked off the muraled ceiling, and the lights in the constellations are burned out. The old New York, New Haven & Hartford Railroad ticket windows have been converted to Off-Track Betting windows. Commercialism and neglect have taken their toll on Grand Central Terminal. A hundred and sixty thousand commuters and a couple of hundred "Amtrakers" pass through it each day and that's it. The Great Silver Fleet, the Shoreline expresses, the Canadian trains . . . all have raced out of the terminal to oblivion. Tracks 34 and 26 handle MU cars now, as easily as any other track does. Assistant Station Master J. W. O'Rourke aptly calls GCT a "big commuter barn." That's it.

With the physical plant of the railroad largely still there to coincide with memories, it's easy to romance over trains and railroading . . . and why not? There is, however, an up-dated version to railroading—another aspect of the "personal vocabulary" I mentioned earlier—a version packed with new technology and equipment, producing greater gross ton-miles than ever, but barely managing a return on investment. Railroading is still the same old (but true) story of the efficiency of the steel-flanged wheel on steel track, but with a new twist. Certainly the evolution of freight cars over the past fifteen years has affected the industry as much as the change to diesel power. I spent several years with ACF demonstrating, leasing, and selling some of the most innovative, sophisticated rail equipment that exists. More and more new-service, built-for-a-job freight cars roll out of the car-builders' shops, and more and more are moving under reporting marks of shipper-owners and private-lease fleets. Bulk liquid and dry commodities, containers, automobiles, auto parts, appliances—a whole new generation of new and different rail cars designed for specific—highly specific—jobs has been altering the very heart of the industry. Center Flow, auto-rack, TTX, jumbo, whale, Versa-Deck, Air Pak, Dyna Bulk, 5 PSI, High-Cube, Hydra-Cushion—this is the new freight-car language. The list of names is endless. Over one fifth of today's railroad freight cars are privately owned! Some photos of the new look in railroading appear in this chapter.

Getting back to my first railroad love, steam, it has a new look, too. Times *have* changed, and for steam maybe they have changed for the better. In the mid to late 60's, most parts of the country became completely diesel-dead-locked, with no steam-relief (fan trips) in sight. The few operating mainline steam locomotives were all in the East, with the exception of an occasional firing-up of Union Pacific's 8444. But in the late 60's, and now in the early 70's, steam has *taken to the road !* Who in the mid-60's would have guessed that a Nickel Plate Berk would reach Kansas City? And what about Canadian Pacific 4-6-2's pounding along the Pennsy main? Or a Reading T-1, in D & H garb yet, entering Montreal—and locking couplers with a CPR 4-6-2 painted Delaware & Hudson? Who, in his wildest of dreams, would have come up with these happenings? In 1965, had I dreamt such fantasies—and made the mistake of sharing them—I would have been looked at with amazement!

Today as I write this, I foresee, over the next half-decade, EMD C-C and B-B-B electric locomotives testing tonnage under wires of the former Penn Central with mechanical people from BN and U.P. on board; I foresee Amtrak operating over their own tracks and, possibly, the development of the first integral-container train system. I wistfully hope for more candor, less legalistic mumbo-jumbo, less politicking, and a consolidation of some of the eighteen—count 'em—labor unions that represent railroad labor. I look forward to the day when the social responsibility of moving commuters will not belong to the railroad, and, of course, I look forward to regulations that will reflect the present time and not the lush days of railroad monopolies. No, I do not want nationalization, but I hope the government will come up with an equitable way to assist in track-upgrading costs as they have assisted in providing the truck competition with fast, grade-separated interstate rights-of-way. Then, my friends, we'd see some real private-enterprise competition at work! I often spend spare moments wondering why we let Penn Central continue . . . and I wonder what would have happened had New York Central picked up B&O . . . and *why* Congress didn't act when PC was shut down by a strike—that is, until GM and others screamed *they* were going to shut down! As I write this, I'm concerned over the fact that 37.4 valuable miles of Lehigh & Hudson River's well-kept rail are considered "excess trackage" by the Department of Transportation, as 10,000-plus tractor-trailers a day pass near my home on the New England Thruway (I-95) . . . and over the fact that much of Lehigh Valley's major trackage is considered "excess" by DOT, even though traffic over the north-south routes involving Lehigh Valley exceeds

90,000 carloads a year! And perhaps what bothers me most is WHY the LV, D &H, L&HR, E-L, and others should pay a penalty for being near Penn Central!

The unions are asking steel-industry wages and benefits with at least a 15 per cent increase every year, *and* a cost-of-living escalator. The Federal Drug Administration, the Federal Railroad Administration, and the Environmental Protection Agency are asking for changes and "improvements" that will cost the industry *at least* $500 million, plus $70 million in recurring annual costs! And OSHA (the Occupational Safety Hazards Act) is starting to knock on the industry's door for even more costly improvements! As I contemplate the railroads' future, I'm comforted by one thought, and that is that *somehow* the trains will continue to run, and those of us who have chosen to include "railroading" in our vocabulary will be fascinated by them, as we always have been.

The following pages of photos include a few "images" of what "railroading" means to me. It is a sampling of the railroad spirit known so intimately by those who work for, or have worked for, the railroad. It is also a sampling of the romantic past, of the recent grandness of pre-Amtrak passenger travel, of today's market-oriented freight equipment—and of nostalgic, vestigial traces of better days.

". . . for his glory is not at all in going, but in being." John Ruskin

Railroad men: a special breed of lordly, grimy heroes who make railroading possible. There exists an intimacy between these men and their machines—impossible to explain to ordinary people. (BALL, N&W, UP)

Any steam railroader will tell you that no two steam locomotives were ever alike—ever! Each had a different personality. All had horizontal firetube boilers, filled with fire, water, and steam, resting on a frame with cylinders, upon wheels—an imposing array of running gear, valve gear, pipes, pumps, and fittings—all integrally related to the harnessing of steam. Yet out of all of this machinery, each steam locomotive had human qualities. (BALL)

Man on the move! Rods flash, eccentrics spin, pistons thrash, the engine heaves and hunts —a pounding blur of crashing steel, guided by a nerveless hand; this marvelous man-made frenzy that is the steam locomotive. (HALE)

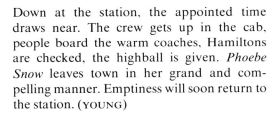

Down at the station, the appointed time draws near. The crew gets up in the cab, people board the warm coaches, Hamiltons are checked, the highball is given. *Phoebe Snow* leaves town in her grand and compelling manner. Emptiness will soon return to the station. (YOUNG)

At this point in history, in the jet and super-highway era, it may seem a little odd praising the "recently vanished American passenger train." However, diesels and stainless steel notwithstanding, most of America's railroads *did* have "passenger train personalities" all their own, right up to Amtrak.

Looking back on some of my train trips just prior to Amtrak's taking over most of the nation's intercity passenger trains: A pullman porter on Santa Fe's *Super Chief* contemplates the days ahead. Below, passengers enjoy scrumptious food aboard Milwaukee's *Afternoon Hiawatha.* At right, the view from the vestibule door on Southern's immaculate *Southern Crescent,* leaning into a Georgia curve. (BALL)

Few changes have saddened me more than the disappearance of America's railroad architecture. When I was a youth, the railroad station ranked in architectural stature with the town's churches. Today, the wooden railroad passenger and freight stations are neglected . . . forgotten. Their "dignity of pleasing decay" is gradually disintegrating into the landscape—going the way of yesterday. (BALL)

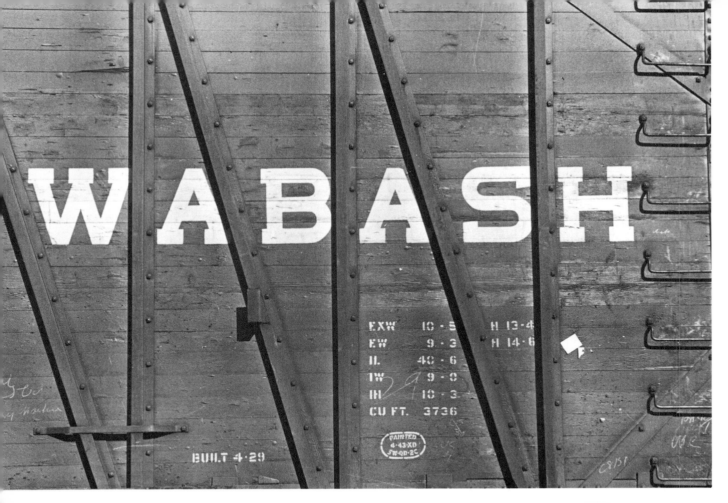

What is it about railroads that is so fascinating, so compelling? Certainly it's more than just locomotives and moving trains. A wooden box car (one that easily meets AAR interchange requirements) is both useful and beautiful; a work of art whether in motion or not—where age is not an excuse for change. (BALL)

Trainload movements. Solid trains of specialized cars rolling through terminals, changing crews on the run, with operating revenues outpacing operating expenses. On this spread, the new look to railroading: patterns of 33,500 gallon LPG tank cars rolling through Louisiana on the MOP; 3,550 cubic feet Center Flow covered hoppers leaving Council Bluffs, Iowa, on the Union Pacific; hopper cars coming and going, to and from the mines, through Roanoke, Va., on the N&W; and stock cars, in drum-roll cadence, moving up through Cajon on the UP. (BALL)

3

SHORTLINES:
AUTUMN MEMORIES

STEINHEIMER

I could very well call this chapter my country journal, as it portrays a part of my life in which the riches that befell me were not only cinder-coated ones. A genuine love affair with the Appalachian country and its people developed during my many bittersweet autumn pilgrimages to this beautiful back country in search of steam. The final curtain had, indeed, gone down on mainline steam railroading. It was only in the off-the-highway countryside that steam could still be seen on a few remaining shortlines, and it was saddening to think that steam whistles across the land were now but poignant dreams . . . ghostly echoes in the corridors of my memory.

Each fall, Indian summer would come, and it would beckon me to adventure. For me, this lovely time did not symbolize the death of the year, but rather the gentle folding of nature's hands in preparation for her long winter's nap—just an intermission between the new year and the return of a new spring. Indian summer was—and is—my favorite time of year. The days are hazy and mild, the sky an incredible blue, the air rich with the smell of burning leaves and woodsmoke, all signaling the last golden days of autumn before the bitterness of winter sets in. When Indian summer came, I'd think of Appalachia and its sweet-smelling hardwood forests and the towering lonely hills that still provided refuge for the last steam locomotives. It was time for me to drive down to the hill country I had grown to love.

On the drive down, long-vanished dreams came alive. The presence of the past could be discerned throughout the landscape. Old farms were tucked among the hills, showing everywhere the evidence of care in working the land. I came to know that West Virginia's pride runs deep—like the coal seams that thread its mountains. It was easy to feel yesterday's union in the Civil War—the hill people's stand against slavery. Hidden away, in the heads of the hollows, little homes stood, with coal smoke drifting straight up from their chimneys. Old mine beds, and scarred mountainsides; loading tipples in the narrow valleys alongside streams. Twisting roads and mining camps, collieries and slag piles. Perhaps forbidding to some, this was the ageless story of men and mountains, where people led a tucked-away, serene life—the way it had always been. It was, to me, a most beautiful land.

Most of my annual stay would be with Grace and Rich Manning in their mountain home outside Dundon. Rich was General Superintendent of the Buffalo Creek & Gauley—in the early 60's the largest all-steam railroad east of the Mississippi, and each fall he would "give" his railroad to about four of us, each at a different time. I'd plan my arrival on the property for late in the afternoon and would head for the Mannings' house. Those evenings at Grace and Rich's are still very much with me. After a garden-fresh supper, we'd wait for the evening mine run, my first look at regular steam railroading in perhaps a year. Two hundred feet from the house and down by the tracks, crickets sang away in the dusty weeds, sounding for all the world like elfin flutes as the twilight deepened. Over the tall dark hills and towards the west, the sun had gone down and the yellow light of evening spread as night approached. The first evening star—a brilliant pinpoint—was joined by others. The mountain wind—sweet, cool, and cleansing—was a soft accompaniment to the quiet flow of the Buffalo Creek. Soon it was dark, and the woods came alive with a symphony of night sounds: more sleepy crickets . . . the pulsing rhythm and snapping of tree toads . . . the lonesome call of a distant whippoorwill . . . the mournful hoot of a solitary owl.

Snug in the West Virginia hills at night, one becomes keenly aware of the seeming closeness of the blue-black sky—a star-studded canopy overhead, illumined by countless millions of diamond-bright stars. "The limitless immensity of space" suddenly ceases to be just a figure of speech and becomes a reality. In this fairyland setting, the banshee-wail of a chime whistle comes through the night air, breaking the thunder of the silence. The distant rumble of the coal train can clearly be heard. Rich calls down from the house to assure me it will be another ten minutes yet. The whistle breaks for a distant grade crossing, and this time its call echoes through the hills. Nature's night symphony has been joined by one of the hill country's most familiar sounds—the tympani of a heavy coal train at night. Again, the whistle shrills hauntingly through the mountains, and the rolling train's echo builds to what sounds like the rush of a tremendous waterfall. I stand still in disbelief and feel an immense inner sadness that this happening is unique—that though those sounds were something I had heard hundreds, really thousands, of times before, now they are heard only here and nowhere else in America. My commonplace West Virginia setting is an anachronistic slice of the past. The screen door bangs shut as Rich comes out to join me. He mentions that the Reds are winning and will wrap up the pennant. Normally, I would care. He stands near the track and listens. "Job Young and Ab Wilson are on the engine—they'll be glad to see you. Did you stop off and see Bobby on the way in?" It didn't seem as if I'd been away for a full year. I had planned to come down between Christmas and New Years and sleep in the caboose, but other plans and bad weather had prevented it. I was glad I had the extra week of vacation now. From somewhere back in the deep forested land came the squeal of flanges. The rumble had turned into a more distinct sound of steel wheels on rail joints, accompanied by the bell of a drifting locomotive. A sharp pull on the whistle-cord—the train was upon us. The engine pounded past, the warmth from her firebox was briefly felt, and out of the dense dark came hopper after hopper after hopper, clanking past, raising dust, and fanning brakeshoe smoke! Ninety-three loads! How I had waited for this night!

In the morning, everything was greyish white. I'd forgotten the mornings. The mountain fog erases all land and surrounds you with its moist embrace until the sun comes burning through. By the time I'm up, Rich is down at the shop, making sure all is well with the firing-up for the day's work. It's a wonder now to walk through the woods. The leaves are wrinkled from the fog, and colored in many hues from a summer of sun. Down the path and out ahead in the grey murk comes the familiar sound of coal being scooped and bailed into a firebox. In the shop yard, one is reminded of a downeast Maine fog that has rolled in off the Atlantic in the afternoon. Shapes and silhouettes disappear and reappear in the denser patches, in this weird, ethereal world.

My buddy Bobby Carruthers greets me with a pail of grease-sticks and an alemite gun—and we go to work! Once again, I hear the thump and sputter of air pumps, steamy pop valves, and the friendly warning not to get my thumb caught in the slot on the gun. I am back in the company of old friends—back in the company I have driven eighteen hours to keep.

The sun shows through the mist now as a yellow disc. A lone cricket sings nearby as the air warms up, and the dew on the Queen Anne's lace shines like pearls in the warm sunlight. #14 pops off and moves out with cylinder-cocks open, bell ringing, and trailing BC&G's only caboose. She'll move on to the main and then back down to the B&O interchange to pick up the empties for the mine at Widen.

Have you ever stood next to, say, the sixtieth hopper car in a string of eighty or ninety, when the engine whistles off and the slack crashes back, past and through the train? It's almost as if you were in an all-metal bowling alley, listening to the pins dropping in an echo chamber. #14 has eighty-nine empties today and her work is cut out for her. With the slack stretched, her great exhaust cracks off the rock ledges in a loud hollow-ringing shout. She'll climb 18.6 miles up through Cressmont and Swandale to the Rich Run mine at Widen. At certain places (if you traverse an almost impassable back road in an automobile to get there), it is possible to walk along next to her when she's really down on her hands and knees.

In the evening, over a couple of beers, there is plenty of steam talk, yes, but you get to know that Rich's road handles just about a million tons of coal a year, plus upwards of 400 loads of lumber. Rich speaks with pride about the 112-lb. rail and the fact that his 2-8-0's can easily handle 3,000 tons over his 0.9 per cent ruling grade. Like all shortlines, the BC&G has a most colorful past, but you won't hear any of that. I happened to know that the last armed robbery of a passenger train in the U.S. had been on the BC&G. And that some of the most violent hassles in the UMW's history took place in organizing the Rich Run mine. Strikes occurred and rail bridges were blown sky-high. A BC&G rail bus was used to smuggle groceries in to those who chose to stay on the job, and armed guards rode the trains. But this was all part of the past. Now my mind was on the present, and the fact that tomorrow I would be riding on, and walking next to, a full-boilered steam locomotive!

Lucius Beebe, writing about the color of shortline railroading, said:

> . . . the essential flavor of a little railroad is so elusive, for all that its rails and rolling stock may be the quintessence of factual reality, that it must be seen and experienced—almost touched—in order to apprehend and faithfully evaluate it. To photograph a short line is not enough; it should be ridden, if possible both head end and in its coaches or caboose, and the truly perceptive reporter will drink whisky with its crew members and talk crops, if such colloquy is within his gift. For a short line is so delicately integrated to the region it serves or transverses, touches so closely the lives of its countryside, that it ranks in importance of function with those of the banker, the leading merchant and the parish man of the cloth.

The little shortlines were built to satisfy a local need, to go where mainline and highway did not go—to a world of watermelon patches, silos, creeks, and sleepy trackside towns. The shortline railroads' enchantment was their local identity, the way they belonged with the land. If you love the countryside, you'll understand how little engines with rattling cars, echoing whistles and friendly waves, coal smoke and eccentric ways were all a part of an off-the-beaten-track, commonplace America that I loved.

Today, I reminisce. I spend a great deal of time happily recalling yesterday's pleasures, and I feel privileged to be able to pass them along. Perhaps I've talked too much about the Buffalo Creek & Gauley. If you were there, you know how I feel. You'll agree that the enchantment was real; you'll agree, also, that Buffalo Creek & Gauley was polished perfection—late in the steam shortline scene. If you were never there, I hope you'll have a taste of its flavor. In the same way, the photographs in this chapter do not comprise the complete chronicle of shortlines, not even that of the Buffalo Creek & Gauley. I've concentrated on a few scenes, and particular locations, that bring back instant recollections of some of the picturesque little railroads that survived into the 50's and 60's—little railroads that, like their mainline cousins, provided wonderful memories that time will not erase. After all, a Kentucky & Tennessee 2-8-2 looming up over the big Yamacraw Viaduct is not easily forgotten, nor is the unsettling clatter of a Brimstone shay grinding through the woods and across the New River. These railroads were the very style and archetype of scores of Appalachian shortlines that once threaded the landscape. Not to be forgotten either, though far from Appalachia, was Mobile & Gulf's untidy and unsophisticated little 2-6-0, making a formidable appearance in this land of diesels, clear up to 1968. Equally indelible in my mind—a Magma Arizona 2-8-0 off in the distance, whisping up a following trace of oil smoke, heading through the desolate desert, and cast against the stark, forbidding Superstitions—a setting that made you fear Apaches would attack at any moment!

I must not close this chapter without mentioning that even as I write these words, one can still drive across the tabletop farm country of Illinois to see steam working in the mills of Northwestern Steel & Wire at Sterling. 1974! Right this minute, amid the general din of the huge mill and the frightful fury of the electric furnace, 0-8-0's toil about, defying eternity, 24 hours a day! The surroundings are ugly, treacherous, too unfriendly for a diesel. Everywhere, rusting scrap and debris lie about, twisted metal and junk; rails half-buried in the ground. Suddenly, a mellow, haunting chime whistle reaches out from somewhere deep within the mill, in beautiful contrast to the dismal surroundings. An 0-8-0 grabs onto a heavy cut of cars and, for a few moments, barks loudly to the heavens, as she was born to do. Another 0-8-0 soon comes into view, and this smoke-filled, unreal setting could be 1940. I'm sure if I were there at this moment, I would be attributing the spectacle to illusion, history books, memories, hopeful wishes—anything other than 1974.

Two Eastern anachronisms: the East Broad Top and the Union Transportation, the East Broad Top being the East's sole surviving narrow-gauge common carrier and the Union Transportation the railroad that operated the Pennsylvania Railroad's last active steam locomotive. Above, East Broad Top's 2-8-2 #17 bursts out of tunnel No. 1 between Fairview and Coles, Pa., with a northbound train. At right, looking for all the world like a Lionel 0-6-0 on a model layout, Union Transportation's Pennsy B-6sb #5244 churns over one of the many timber bridges along the 19-mile New Jersey line. (RONFOR, BALL)

The East Broad Top was chartered in 1856 with the completion of its three-foot main from the Pennsylvania Railroad at Mount Union to the coal deposits at Robertsdale in 1874. The line once operated over 60 miles of tracks with no fewer than eight branches and continued its operations until April 1956 when the coal business was terminated. The beauty and charm of the railroad stems from the unspoiled countryside, heavy traffic for narrow gauge, and out-of-the-way development of the nearby natural resources. Rocky Ridge, Sideling Hill, Rock Hill Furnace are names along the route that tell part of the story.

At the upper left, one of the line's standard Baldwin 3-foot gauge 2-8-2's—in this case, the 17—approaches a grade crossing, northbound at Shirleysburg, Pa., one month before the last coal train would operate. At left, #14's tender is loaded at Orbisonia, while above, #17 chugs over Aughwick Creek with a train for Mount Union on a typically dreary March day in 1956. Happily, there is a good ending to this story. The railroad was sold to Nick Kovalchick of the Kovalchick Salvage Company. Several miles and pieces of equipment were kept intact and on August 13, 1960, the railroad was reopened for tourist operations—to be operated in the authentic manner of old. (BALL, BALL, RONFOR)

All that commotion above is the daily run of Graham County's Shay #1925. Engineer Ed Collins and fireman Posey Davis get 'er cranked up on the run from Robbinsville to Topton, N.C., bevel gears churnin', universals whirlin', cylinders pumpin' and whatever else it takes. The surrounding virgin hardwood setting is in the beautiful Nantahala Gorge. On the opposite page, Graham County's #1925 switches at Topton, and later departs (backing) with its train. (RON-FOR)

"The first steam enjun I ever seen, I was a kid. I gone from watchin' to workin' on 'em. . . . That shovelin' could bend a feller over pretty good."

At left, the BC&G folks relax at the Dundon interchange, waiting for the B&O to bring in the empties.

Below left, hostler Bobby Carruthers walks around #14, checking her out, before the day's trip up to Rich Run Mine. Earlier in the morning (above), the fire is being built up in #14; the beautiful cloak of mountain mist dissipating into the air. These immaculate locomotives are representative of the way Buffalo Creek & Gauley kept things up to the end. (BALL)

"Number 14 is still like a young 'un. She'll outlive all of us."

Above, the two B&O GP-9's that brought the empties down from Grafton lay over on the Charleston line while #14 pumps up the train. To the left, the whole crew—one way or another—sees to it that they get some of that fresh mountain air on the climb up to Widen. To the right, and on another day, #14 departs Dundon, fighting for a foothold, slipping, and sending a great boiling pillar of smoke into the sky. (BALL)

"The coal railroads I reckon' have all gone 'cept the Buffalo Creek. Guess our day will come. . . ."

At left—and the reason for it all—hopper cars are shoved and spotted under the tipple at Widen, loaded and made up into a train. Anywhere else in 1963, such a hard-working mainline steam locomotive would seem like a harsh intrusion from out of the past. On this page, a close-up look at the mine, and a deep woods vignette of the return train, heading for Dundon. Oh yes, "our day" did come for the BC&G: December 30, 1963. (BALL)

Once every month, the East Tennessee & Western North Carolina changed steam locomotives—that is, dropped the fire in one and lit up the other. It was a rare occasion when both 2-8-0's were under steam at the same time. Such a day took place in August 1967, when #207 and #208 were photographed (at left) in Johnson City. Below, the comings and goings of Kentucky & Tennessee's 2-8-2 #12, formerly (and presently) Southern's #4501. At right, K&T 2-8-2 #10 puts in an appearance in lovely back country along the ten-mile line. (BALL, WHEELIHAN, WHEELIHAN)

Georgia Pacific's Shay #19 does some routine railroading back in the forests along the Lilly Fork. The road shared some trackage with the Buffalo Creek & Gauley, but unlike the high and dryer BC&G, often found its operations changed without notice! (RONFOR)

Kentucky & Tennessee's 2-8-2 #12 completes the post-card picture, rambling across the graceful Yamacraw bridge on an otherwise dreary day, March 1963. Not known at the time, this engine would be saved for future generations to enjoy. (WHEELIHAN)

Runnin' hellbent (6 mph) for the Southern Railway connection, Brimstone's stalwart Shay #35 clatters out of the woods and across the New River with coal from Little Creek. This highfalutin' Tennessee short line was about the last home for the geared Shay locomotive, and provided action (of sorts) for steam-starved rail fans in the 60's. More to my liking (above), the 24-mile Mississippian Railway and its two 68-ton ex-Frisco 2-8-0's. On this day, the train is in the hands of Frank Carlisle and #77, getting out of Amory. In two days, brother Jim Carlisle will do the honors in his engine—2-8-0 #76. (RONFOR, COLLINS)

Mobile & Gulf No. 97. No 90 mph here; no Valhalla at Vaughan; certainly no Casey Jones on the payroll—just honest to goodness railroading along M&G's 11-mile main. On the far left, No. 97 makes a formidable exit from the GM&O interchange at Buhl, high-balls (8 mph) through Mose Henly's back yard (above), and eventually disappears into the Alabama back country. Alas, on August 25, 1970, this last-in-the-land common carrier steam operation came to a quiet end. (BALL)

When Betty Grable was the locker-door pin-up girl in America and the Andrews Sisters were singing *Boogie Woogie Bugle Boy from Company B,* the scenes on these pages were typical of everyday America. Today, Fred Astaire and Ginger Rogers would certainly not be featured on the marquee of the local Sterling, Illinois, movie theater, but down on the streets along the railroad tracks, little change would be noticed. Today, as one stands along Northwestern Steel & Wire's tracks, hefty 0-8-0's come forth with dreams of the past, switching the mill and seldom stopping long enough for a time exposure such as the one above. (BALL)

In the Divine Order of Things, these locomotives should probably not even exist today. There always has to be a *last* in any category, but Northwestern Steel and Wire's operating 0-8-0's *continue* to be the last with no real end in sight! On this spread are scenes from some of my more memorable visits to Sterling, including the blizzard of February 1965, when Mother Nature all but did me in—I finally had to seek refuge in an abandoned shack! (BALL)

Out in the desert, at the base of the stark Superstitions, not much survives in the arid climate—some scorpions, snakes, and saguaro cactus, but little else. The land looks much as it did when the Apaches had their last war party. The 30-mile copper-hauling Magma Arizona Railroad featured on this spread managed to "survive," operating with steam from 1915 to 1968, when diesels finally took over. Of the three steam locomotives the road owned, only one, #5, shown here, was built new for the railroad.

At the immediate left, the "down train" from Superior to Magma slowly approaches the Desert Wells tank, midway along the line. The view from the top (lower left) clearly shows desert plant life thriving, evidence of a recent rain storm. At right, the 1922 Alco comes off its own rails and onto the Southern Pacific at Christmas Tree Jct., framed in a bit of 20th-century railroading. Below, and working upgrade toward Superior, the copper-painted smokebox on #5 leads the train on a charge across one of the many dry-wash trestles. (BALL)

A brief look at four shortlines in steam in the West. On the left page, West Side Lumber's 3-foot gauge Shay #9 heading the down train through Tuolumne, California, in the dark hours of late night. To its right, in the early morning, Feather Rivers three-truck Shay heads toward Feather Falls in 1963. This was California's last steam-powered railroad. Above, an early October snow and cold weather add zest to the passage of Great Western's eastbound train out of Loveland, Colorado, in 1968. The locomotive on this glorious day (cold-footed day!) is 2-8-0 #60. At the immediate left, a Northern Pacific 4-6-0 mirrors its goings, working an eastbound freight on the Camus Prairie Railroad near Kamiah, Idaho, in 1951. (STEINHEIMER, WITTENBORN, BALL, GRIFFITHS)

223

4

FAN FARE

How many times have I reminded myself that those of us who had it so good ought not to complain! Recently, while en route to see Southern's 4501 for the first time, my friend Walt remarked about her carrying a canteen—an obvious and disdainful reference to the fact that while in regular service she never had an auxiliary tender. It bothered him that this locomotive was not being operated "the way it was supposed to be." Come to think of it, it made me unhappy, too. I recalled the days she was just plain black, with handsome Gothic gold numerals on her flanks. Why, she should be heading a long swaying string of merchandise! As I thought about these things, suddenly time seemed to roll back. It could have been 1940. For that matter, we could be heading down into North Carolina to watch Saluda's 4.7 per cent under steam! More realistically, it could be the mid-50's, and just another trip when we were combing the countryside for those last steam survivors. Images of this treasured past were all at once hauntingly close. That was to be expected . . . it is the bittersweet experience a fan trip brings on. No, we mustn't complain—a fire has been laid on the grate and 4501 is alive and well.

Thank God, a few diehard railroad presidents refused to let the Iron Horse disappear! President Harry P. Murphy of Burlington was one of them. In the 1960's, when steam was all but a memory across the land, out of the shops of Burlington came examples of Q's finest, to teach the young good things. And out of the shops of Reading came some of their big T-1's—certainly the biggest and best ever to haul Reading's Rambles. Joe Fisher, Reading's president, recognized the big locomotive's p.r. value, and he couldn't have found a better way to capitalize on people's nostalgia. In the motor city, Grand Trunk was not about to lose touch with the past—not completely. GTW 4-8-4's which had been lovingly stored would be fired up to handle capacity crowds that wanted to ride behind steam. And, out of the woods and towns and cities all across America came the steam-starved multitudes to witness once more a stirring pageant of smoke, steel, and steam. Those few railroads which brought back the long-vanished object of our affection became famous overnight, and the names of many of their top people became household words.

The first railroad excursion is said to have taken place in the 1850's, and other excursions followed thereafter in regular succession. But according to railroad periodicals, excursion fever was catching on in earnest just as the Great Depression hit. Like some investors, the public-excursion business never really recovered. *Railway Age*, in its issue of March 9, 1935, editorialized on the importance of the railroads' using "a reasonable degree of showmanship" in presenting their locomotives, cars, and facilities to the general public. The editorial went on to mention the undoubtedly large but dormant interest on the part of the public, just waiting for "a challenge on the part of the railroads" to bring it to life. Perhaps most important was the fact that the pressure for better public relations came not only from the rail buff, but also from people who had a general interest in the welfare of the railroad industry. The attitude that prevailed was perhaps best summed up in a letter published in April of the same year in *Railway Age*. I would like to quote its still-timely message. Remember, it was written early in 1935!

The writer might be considered a "hobbyist," having been interested in, and fascinated by railroad operation in all its forms since childhood. Inculcated in this interest is a very healthy desire to see the railroads live and prosper and a feeling amounting to personal resentment at seeing their revenues depleted and even many of their lines abandoned as the result of an invasion by other less dependable forms of transportation which are not even self-supporting—and to add insult to injury, even derive advantages to the tune of millions of dollars from the taxes which the railroads are compelled to pay.

I am not going to add myself to the endless list of individuals who see fit to criticize the railway systems, but I do think that they would be greatly benefited, both in publicity and revenue, if they would give some recognition in the form of encouraging the inspection of their facilities and rolling stock to these hobbyists, most of whom are not railroad employees, for which reason their opinions and views would not be considered as biased as those of actual employees. *I for one, let my interest go to the extent that I buy my milk from a company which ships it on the railroad, where it belongs, which practice also applies to the coal I purchase —and for which I pay several dollars more a ton—rather than patronize a bootleg trucker.* Of course, I am a very small consumer, but if a large number of the public were recognized and encouraged, the benefits, both direct and indirect, would be great. One of the causes for the great success of the motor car is advertising where it does the most good—and the railroads should take this to heart.

I debated over whether I should repeat so much of this letter. Obviously, economic factors and modes of distribution have changed, but I cannot but feel that, with only a few changes, this letter, written nearly forty years ago, could be sent today. Its theme rings so true!

Al Kalmbach, during the same period, spoke of "men of influence" as the ones engaged in model railroading, while the railroads were "not overdoing themselves" to be courteous and helpful even though they were receiving "valuable and genuinely enthusiastic backing" from the modelers. So much for history. Contemporary overtones as well as nostalgic remembrances emerge from these statements, and I wanted to share them with you.

When steam was becoming history—and everyone knew it—pressure was brought on the railroads to keep the dying era alive by presenting outstanding examples of steam locomotives to museums, civic groups, towns and villages, and railroad collections. For some reason, an 0-6-0 more often got the paint, while the 4-8-4 got the torch. Sometimes I'm ashamed to have to tell a young person that the 2-8-0 in the park was, indeed, a freight engine. If only it were a 2-10-4! Nevertheless, there *are* some fine locomotives that were saved. Special thanks go to some of the latter-day saints—the Southern Railway, Union Pacific, Canadian National—who are now maintaining the steamy side of their personalities.

To go over a bit of history, the Burlington dieselized in January 1959. By March 1960, all railroads were officially dieselized. Although some railroads are now accommodating steam and in many cases rebuilding steam for active service, I regard the Burlington as the one railroad that did not close its roundhouse doors on steam when that March day passed. Burlington ran a steam excursion for the Illini Railroad Club on July 3, 1955, and managed to operate twenty-one—count 'em, TWENTY-ONE—different locomotives of various classes before economic factors forced the retirement of Ola #4960 on July 17, 1966. On that last trip, the Illini Railroad Club presented those aboard with a "Heritage of Steam Historical Certificate" for their "interest in the great tradition of American railroading, and the colorful steam era in particular." I'm proud to have been aboard.

The photographs that follow tell only part of the tremendous steam revival story. I wish there were space for more. I have included the more recent trips and the locomotives that have meant the most to me. I have even included a few diesels, since steam, believe it or not, no longer has a corner on the fan-trip market. (Do you suppose we'll someday have a farewell-to-geeps fan trip? Farewell to the diesel?)

Finally, no chronicle of steam fan trips would be complete without mentioning two men I have the privilege of calling friends. They are Graham Claytor and Ross Rowland, neither of whom needs an introduction. The Southern Railway's great success story is well known, from the pages of *Fortune, Trains,* and *The Wall Street Journal,* and from investment analysts and the stock-market quotations. The Cinderella story of the High Iron Company, however, is not so well known. For some reason, the High Iron Company has not really received the public acclaim it deserves, although because of it I have relished hours in the cabs and out under the cinders of some mighty wonderful engines! Without Ross Rowland's High Iron family, my son would not have seen steam on freight, nor would he have ridden on the rear end of "Brothers Two", behind steam. Nor would his father have had the chance to scoop coal in the late 60's! I thought I had seen the last of those days-in-the-cab back on the B&O and the Buffalo Creek & Gauley! Well, now for a little HICO biography!

In 1966, Ross Rowland could no longer suppress his love for steam locomotives. While most of us mourned and took up modeling, Ross went to Nelson Blount at Steamtown and the CNJ to see if steam could once again be operated on the "High Iron." Thanks to typical Rowland brass and persuasion, the High Iron Company was formed, and in October 1966, ex CPR 4-6-2 #127 ran from Elizabeth to Jim Thorpe, Pa., with a capacity load. Everything worked! During the following two years, mainline excursions were run with the 127, George Hart's ex CPR 4-6-2's #1286 and #1238 and Strasburg's 2-10-0 #90. The bug had bitten Ross, and he quietly went to work looking for a super-power locomotive that could run long and hard—and fast! Ross, like most fans, knew the Steamtown collection and made up his mind that, somehow, Lima's big Berkshire #759 had to return to mainline service. In March 1968, he made a formal proposal to a rather stunned Steamtown board, and the fence came tumbling down! To throw in a few names, Wes Camp, Ross's locomotive man, examined the locomotive and paperwork and gave an enthusiastic go-ahead. John Rehor, then on the N&W from the NKP, heard about the project from a photographer friend, Don Wood. Rehor contacted Paul Percy, estimating engineer for Lima, and worked out the lease of a stall in the old Nickel Plate roundhouse in Conneaut, Ohio (a previous home for 759). Rehor put Wes and Ross in touch with Dale ("Pop") Moses, who had worked on 759 during her construction. Pop flew to Keene, N.H., to look over the white-lined 759. Within one week—*one week*—Wes, Pop, and Hank Webber got her out and started the long journey back to Conneaut. The only tools they carried (in the cab) were a pipe wrench and hammer. Wes followed in his car, checking on such things as wooden half-cylinder heads that were bolted on to reduce wear in the cylinders. The only mishap that occurred was when the sheet-metal rain-cover on the stack blew off from the back cylinder pressure. The train kept going! At Conneaut, the press was waiting, as were volunteers and a yard diesel to shove the big S-2 into her stall. Dale became the chief locomotive adviser (he knew 759 in his sleep), and Joe Karal joined as boilermaker. Day and night, Wes, Joe, Pop, Lee Smith, Bob Bartone, Doyle McCormack, and others swarmed over 759, overlooking nothing. On August 30, 1968—only a little over two months later—the big Berk locked couplers with a caboose and sprinted through three round trips to Thornton Jct., Pa., on the old Nickel Plate main. On September 8, 1968, a dream came true for Ross Rowland when a "brand new" 2-8-4 was dedicated at the Conneaut yard office. Six Vermont winters, white lines, and grey Steamtown paint were faded memories. The 759 was very much alive!

Several photographs that follow show this great star at work on High Iron trips, including one of the Golden Spike Centennial Limited, on which the 759 ran from Harmon, N.Y., to Kansas City. But the behind-the-scenes dedication of the High Iron Company cannot be portrayed in pictures. I haven't yet mentioned Don Smith (Ross's longest-serving full-time employee), Andy Adams, Bob Lorenz, Russ Shipman, Charlie Strunk, Keith and Ron Muldowney—all good friends—who also worked hard to make mainline steam a reality. Today, when I can see Union Pacific's 8444, or the 2102 (302), or 759, I rejoice that there are still a few iron horses that can kick their iron hooves in the face of a diesel!

BALL

In *Portrait of the Rails*, I cited statistics such as in 1934 there were 11,266 2-8-0's, 9,830 2-8-2's, and 2,054 2-10-2's on the nation's rails. Just prior to, during, and after World War II, some impressive, modern 4-8-4's were built—a total of about 1,000 of these beautiful machines gracing the nation's rails. When the diesels came, the Burlington kept most of its 36 Northerns in standby service and then saw to it that some would be saved for fan-trip service. I would like to take this opportunity to thank the Burlington for keeping steam alive for several post-diesel years.

To the left, a sight to stir men's souls as big, well-groomed Burlington 4-8-4 #5632 accelerates out of Chicago's Union Station with a fan trip to LaCrosse, Wisconsin, the consist obviously as nice as that on most name trains. At right, an early morning workaday glimpse at the big Northern being readied at Clyde Roundhouse for another fan trip out of the windy city. Below, a mile out of Union Station, a going-away panorama of what sentimentalists believe standard railroading should look like! Up front, Burlington's 64" drivered freight 2-8-2 #4960. No matter, the "feeling" is very much there. (HARWOOD, BALL, BALL)

For a moment, a glorious moment, Burlington's spritely 4960 holds down the main, east of Aurora, heading home to Chicago with a trainload of happy riders. I stood next to the three-track main, awed by a beautiful western sky. Far off in the distance, 4960's Nathan chime cried out. A headlight and smoke appeared on the horizon. I'll never forget her approach and the apprehension I had that she'd stop smoking, but she pounded past, leaving a beautiful smoky trail—and my pounding heart! On this page, the hostler at Clyde Roundhouse rides 4960's pilot onto the turntable. There's snow on the ground and a frosty cold, crystal-clear day ahead—perfect weather for a fan trip! (BALL)

The traditional approach to rail photography is the ¾ action shot or "wedge" as it is popularly called. Lucius Beebe standardized this style, waiting at trackside along the ballast. With fan trips, I have tried to avoid the wedge, even though it often becomes a necessity when on the run, leaping down to the tracks from a pursuing chase by automobile! One such shot appears at left, as Dick Jensen's ex-GTW Pacific highballs an excursion over the Grand Trunk Western out of Chicago on September 17, 1967. At right, Canadian National's 4-8-4 #6218 startles the pigeons, getting underway out of Chicago with another excursion over the GTW to South Bend, Indiana on November 20, 1966. Below, Burlington's #4960 appears from out of the fog in Riverside, Illinois, on a westbound trip to Denrock, on April 26, 1965. (BALL)

As in the U.S., Canadian steam operations ceased in 1960. I was fortunate enough to be in the cab of 4-8-4 #6153 on September 4, 1960, on what was officially billed "the end of steam on CNR." Happily, the official retirement didn't last and we've enjoyed seeing 4-8-4's 6167 and 6218, along with "bullet-nosed Betty," 4-8-2 #6060, carrying on CNR's 124-year-old tradition of steam railroading. Pictured are three "steamy Canadian cousins." At left, on perhaps the most colorful steam special operated, ex-GTW 4-6-2 #5629 slips her 73″ drivers, working the July 4th circus train from Baraboo to Milwaukee through the hilly Wisconsin farmland. Above, on Grand Trunk Western rails east of Valparaiso, Indiana, the road foreman calls for up-the-line conditions, moving #6218 light toward Ft. Huron. Below, CNR's current performer, #6060, crosses the Richelieu River Bridge at Otterburn, Quebec. (BALL, BALL, ZIMMERMANN)

"The Reading Railroad Will Operate Giant Steam Locomotive," so said a press release from the company in October 1959. After two years of nothing but diesels back east, this news was understandably met with celebrated disbelief! Of all the railroads, little old Reading would fire up one of its huge freight-hauling class T-1's for the fans. Unbelievable! And so the story goes: the first "Iron Horse Ramble" left Philadelphia for Shamokin, Pa., on October 25, 1959, three weeks after the announcement. 4-8-4 #2124 did the honors, with sixteen cars carrying 970 joyous passengers!

The Reading T-1 was a coal hauler—certainly not a glamour puss! In fact, until October 1959, the 2100's were relatively unknown, unappreciated. We soon found out that a T-1 was a fabulous piece of machinery. At the immediate right, two T-1's, #2124 and #2100, depart Shamokin, Pa., on a beautiful October 15, 1960, boosters cut in for the steep grade ahead. Below, the original T-1, #2100, is on the point of a trip to Gettysburg in May 1963, shown leaving Norristown, Pa. On the left-hand page, scenes from a February 1972 trip from Baltimore to Hagerstown with privately owned ex-Reading #2102. top, approaching Smith's Station, Pa., at speed, and below left, striding along west of Westminster, Maryland. (BALL)

Amid the world of high-pulsed, supercharged diesels, Southern has seen to it that the young will understand the urge that made boys leave the farm and that the old will remember the lure of the in-the-middle-of-the-night whistles that called to them. My salute to Southern, and thanks to friends Graham Claytor, Jim Bistline, Bill Purdy, Jim Geeslin, and Pier Clifford for their parts in making steam a living legend.

On the left page, Southern's #4501 heads east out of the sunset, over Christiansburg Mountain near Elliston, Va., on an NRHS excursion over N&W rails. At the top of this page, and a day after the NRHS trip, September 20, 1970, #4501 crosses the James River at Natural Bridge, Va., immortalized in a classic portrait by Victor Hand. At right, the diesel-era problems of getting water to the iron horse.

Two other stars in Southern's steam stable are Consolidation's #630 and #722, formerly East Tennessee & Western North Carolina, formerly Southern Railway. As with Mikado #4501, they have been welcomed back home to Southern's rails. Why, what other railroad can boast of a Master Mechanic-Steam on its payroll—in 1974? (HAND, HAND, YOUNG)

I have never liked calling a particular steam locomotive a "fan trip engine" simply because one of a species has been preserved for excursion purposes. The popular connotation for such engines is usually an *antique* steam engine. Certainly, Union Pacific's 8444 could hold down any of *today's* timetable schedules if asked to do so, and this grand lady—the finest example of steam power running—can show people what a modern steam locomotive is all about! Usually shown at speed, I have chosen two slightly different views of this big 4-8-4. Above, on Sherman Hill in a 28-inch blizzard, and at right, ready to leave Laramie, Wyo. Both photographs were taken on February 20, 1971. (BALL)

At left, ex-Nickel Plate Berkshire #759 hammers up the Hudson on the former New York Central with the *Golden Spike Centennial Limited* on May 3, 1969. The location is Break Neck tunnel.

To the right, #759 heads up the Hudson, across the Peekskill inlet, after doing honors on High Iron's *Mohawk Valley Limited* to Niagara Falls and return on October 12 and 13, 1971. Below, a scene of vanishing American heritage. The 759, built by Lima in 1944, comes off the Lurgan, Pa., wye after shoving a Western Maryland freight from Hagerstown. In the background, a palatial triple-decker bank barn, itself a product of the late eighteenth century. (BALL, BALL, YOUNG)

The "Lima Lady" in her three roles: pulling freight, hauling excursions, shoving freight. Above, #759 puts on a grand show, passing the old creamery at Tunnel, N.Y., on August 18, 1972, on her "last run" to Steamtown. At left, super power on the move out of Jim Thorpe, Pa., on July 15, 1971. At right, orders are handed up to the train and engine crew at Hagerstown, Md., on a Reading freight on February 16, 1971. Of all the personal thrills #759 has provided me, none will compare with that February morning in Hagerstown, watching 1970-era freight cars on the run, being shoved by a smoke-belching, hooked-up steam locomotive on the rear! (YOUNG, YOUNG, BALL)

Most of us know that Delaware and Hudson celebrated its 150th anniversary in April 1973 with a super steam trip from Colonie, N.Y. to Montreal and return. Two locomotives were used: Steamtown's ex-CPR 4-6-2 #127 and ex-Reading T-1 #2102. Both engines were "D&H-ized" into #653 and #302, respectively. What most of us will never know is the behind-the-scenes ingenuity, squabbles, and work that went into changing the engines' appearances—such things as #302 sporting a tank car dome, rim of a bus tire, diesel headlight.

At upper left, ex-CPR 4-6-2, sporting D&H-style smoke lifters and re-numbered #653, departs Saratoga Springs, N.Y., on the return lap of its pre-anniversary trip shakedown run from Colonie. At left, a month after D&H's successful celebration, flat-faced T-1 No. 302 stomps across the bridge into Hancock, N.Y., with High Iron's *New York State Express* over the E-L to Binghamton, N.Y. Above, the complete 22-car train is seen along the Delaware five miles north of Callicoon, N.Y. On the rear is "Splendid Spirit," painted red, white, and blue, telling of the coming American Freedom Train. (BALL)

249

Many fan trips are run to pay last respects to a locomotive or a class of locomotive slated for retirement and, as I mentioned in the text, this honor is not always given to steam. On the left, three Alco PA diesels grace fabled Starrucca Viaduct on an Erie Lackawanna "PA Farewell" fan trip in 1963. At right, the slanted prow of Rock Island's E-6 is shown from a weed's-height view as the diesel leaves Chicago on the "Golden Rocket" commemorating EMD's 50th anniversary, September 10, 1972. Below, New York Central's 60-year-old "Ives tinplate" S-motor #110 rolls an ERA excursion down the Harlem Division through Hartsdale, N.Y., on November 13, 1966. (YOUNG, BALL, PICKETT)

5

CHANGING
OF THE GUARD

BALL

Like so many others, I could hardly believe it when the only choice for the train-watching photographer became diesel. It didn't matter whether it was EMD, Baldwin, Alco, Fairbanks Morse, or any other diesel. They were all the same! True, when I was a boy I did have my favorite paint schemes on the first E's, and I was enraptured when a new diesel streamliner came to town, but their likes were unique—each one a special occasion, a temporary phenomenon. Certainly nothing more than a sidelight to the steam railroad scene. When I became older, of course I knew this assessment had been wrong. Things *were* changing. Unbelievably, steam was on the wane, and it was time to photograph all the steam locomotives I could find! At trackside, when a diesel showed up instead of steam, I felt gypped, cheated—and this type of occurrence began to happen regularly. Soon I was heading back to town— back to the tower, the station, the roundhouse, the dispatcher's office—looking for lineups with steam on them. The day came when there was no longer a need for the lineup—let alone railroad photography. The diesel had taken over.

It must have been summer 1964, long after steam, when I returned to the Point Pleasant station on the New York & Long Branch. I was visiting friends at the beach for the weekend and decided to "reminisce" a little before heading for home. After all, the last time I had walked that platform I could pat the cylinder of a K-4. It was time to go back, but it was so many years later, I didn't expect to see much.

I was surprised to find a younger fellow waiting at platform's end with a new 35mm camera, and, naturally, conversation started up. He talked of PA's and E's, F-7's and geeps—a totally new world to me—and seemed only slightly interested in what I had to say about K-4's. Never mind, I thought. I knew what it had been like, and he was the loser. A single-note air horn sounded (off-key at that!), and my acquaintance began to go through the last-minute camera-checking ritual that I am so familiar with. Two diesels rumbled up the track and past us, stopping with a seven-car train. My young friend ran down past the engines. I can't claim to have been so ignorant that I didn't know the units to be Baldwins (as I'm recalling this, I turned to Al Stauffer's *Pennsy Power II*, to the FM section, to get the model number—I'll never learn!) and of the "shark-nose" variety, but I certainly didn't realize that only Pennsy had them, and that they too were nearing the end of the line—as the K-4's were when I had last been at Point Pleasant. And I did get a good look at these diesels' size. They really *were* big, and impressive, and they had racy lines smacking of Raymond Loewy's T-1 steam influence. Down the ballast ran my photographer-friend. The signal was given and the big Baldwins revved up and headed out of town. Down the track and near him, a sizable trace of oily exhaust pushed up at transition, and I hoped he caught it in his picture. The train was soon out of sight. How I wished I had not left the camera in the car!

I had never thought back on that day until I started writing this book. I did have the camera in the car, and I did drive back to Bay Head Jct. to photograph those big shark-nosed Baldwins whose impending doom my friend had told me of—in the same way I'd told others about the demise of steam. I took the time to pace the big units off, look at their impressive trucks and barn-shaped, tapered roof lines. I found myself regretting that there weren't more of these big chisel-nosed racers on the head end of varnish. I imagined silver trucks and the elegant striped lines of New York Central on them. I envisioned B&O and Missouri Pacific paint—what they would have looked like—and I wondered how many similar units had passed me while I waited for Pennsy steam, camera in hand.

Since that day, the years have raced by. In the light of my love for railroading, I've often thought about the diesel. I've tried to accept it from a purely aesthetic point of view, but have found that hard to do. I've tried to accept the fact that some rail photographers find tremendous satisfaction— perhaps even a thrill—in photographing diesels. This I have honestly not been able to do. The only external evidence of a diesel's power (or inner heart), are the cab windows where engineer and fireman sit, and the grilles and louvers which reflect the nature and positioning of the mechanisms inside. The diesel's function is, of necessity, hidden from view (after all, the transformation of fuel into kinetic energy has to take place inside a weatherproof housing). With steam, the beauty was honest, naked.

A month after my Point Pleasant jaunt, ACF transferred me to Chicago, where I could let Burlington's #5632 and #4960 set at rest my apprehensions about diesels!

More years have gone by, and now even the colorful early diesels are gone. Occasionally, I look through some of my movies and slides and find myself pausing to look at the bold and brightly painted diesels that once headed this nation's crack trains. It's crazy, but if some railroad, or group, painted up one of the very few remaining E-6's or PA's in, say, the original maroon-and-gold livery of Pennsy, or the red-flagged blue, grey, and white of Wabash, or the maroon, red, and gold of GM&O, I know I would go to see it. Perhaps I feel that way because the colorfully painted diesels take me back to the era when they were nudging aside steam, when they symbolized the bold upswing of the railroads with a colorful grandeur all their own. The original diesels, and their streamlined trains, were splashy, captivating—a novelty on the railroad scene. Each was associated with a crack train. Mind you, I said a crack train. *Rocket* meant maroon-and-red diesels on stainless steel, nothing else. *Eagle* meant blue-and-cream diesels with portholes and matching cars. And *Zephyr*—well, we all know what *Zephyr* meant, even up through the fluted stainless steel E-5's.

In the evolution of diesel motive power, the replacements for these early diesels came in somber hues, packing more refinements and greater horsepower, and dressed in utilitarian garb. "Second-generation diesels" is what we called them. Their builders gave them the seemingly contradictory name of "road switcher." I suspect few railroad men realized how accurate that term really was.

In the first chapter, I lauded "my decade"—1950 to 1960—from the standpoint of railroading variety. The absolute end of steam would certainly go down as *the event* in that decade, but I would have to mark the appearance and ensuing development of the hood-unit (second-generation) diesel as the not-far-behind, second-most-important event. I want to submit that, for me, the hood-unit diesel "snuck through the back door." Perhaps it did with most train-watchers. My first encounter with this utilitarian breed took place one day in Bonner Springs, Kansas, while I was waiting to shoot Union Pacific's train No. 39 and its 4-6-2. Three black, red, and white Rock Island geeps appeared on the horizon with a westbound hotshot. They were colorful with their tri-colored striping and silver trucks, but they definitely lacked the grace of the cab units. My initial impression was that these units meant business; that there would be more of them on the railroad scene. Little did I realize that what I had seen would soon become *the universal locomotive*, replacing not only what was left in steam, but the F's on freight, the E's on varnish—and everything in between! Road switcher is what they called them.

Once railroading gets in your blood, there is no way to get it out! Guys who used to shoot steam went back to trackside to try color on the early diesels. Others waited and then returned with the visceral feeling that they were being challenged by the hoods—that the many moods of steam could be simply *documented,* but the diesel had to be *portrayed* in its railroad role. The younger generation rail photographer had to start from scratch. I believe the result has been a more innovative rail-photo journalism . . . more feeling for the subject, better composition, an intense awareness of the complete picture. I marvel at what today's fans capture on film, what they seem to feel and understand. I wish more of them had been around when steam was with us, but I'm happy the interest continues.

Many of the pictures in this chapter were "grab shots" while waiting for steam. Most, however, are honest attempts to document diesel railroading. (Ironically, the biggest selection of contributors' photos that I had to choose from were diesels!) I only hope that in the space allowed I've included the right ones. Obviously a whole book would be needed to cover the diesel story (and I started out by saying they all looked the same!).

Yes, I have made my peace, late in the game, with diesels. In 1966, I was introduced, at trackside, to what GM&O called their "Mass-ter Movement train," or simply put—four 3,000 horsepower SD-40's running the wheels off 126 loads of coal from Percy, Illinois, to Joliet, for Commonwealth Edison. In 1967, three Union Pacific Alco Century 855's totaling 16,500 hp roused me at dawn from Cheyenne's Hitching Post Motel, to a chase-by-car in my pajamas that proved in vain. A year later, I got my first look at the awesome, desolate country between Redlands and Beaumont, California—being trampled upon by over 20,000 horsepower worth of GE diesels on a Southern Pacific unit train. I knew I had made peace with the diesels! As I write this, I eagerly await the developing of some film I just shot of four Lehigh Valley Alco Century 628's assaulting the Poconos with a noisy vegeance. Diesels . . . there are times while waiting at trackside when I'm geared up for them—inspired—and suddenly, a glinting moment of sunshine on nearby weeds, a smell or sound, or a vigorous breath of fresh air will spontaneously rekindle a memory from the past—perhaps the thundering approach of a B&O T-4 coming at me, fast! Engineer waving a gloved hand, smoke billowing, bell ringing, as if it were only yesterday . . . and then the heavy silence as I yearn to hear a whistle. Air horns and droning diesel engines all at once interrupt; I find myself dissatisfied with the empty presence of today's trains. The sunlight, the smell, the vigorous breath are there—but that wonderful moment of my life has passed. Diesels . . .

BALL

On the following pages, I've tried to cover the diesel's transition . . . the gradual changeover from the graceful cab units to the utilitarian hood units that now head our trains.

The diesels on these two pages once headed plush trains like the *Pine Tree* and *Minute Man*, *Super Chief* and *El Capitan*, *Broadway* and *Admiral*. Late in the game, a few of the remaining species were relegated to secondary trains and commuter runs. Items: Boston & Maine's local train from Berlin, N.H., along the Ammonoosuc (at left) behind a beautiful E-7; Santa Fe's *Grand Canyon Limited* (below) the day before Christmas 1967, nearing Fullerton, Cal.; and Pennsy Baldwin sharks and E-7's on Long Branch commuter trains at Bayhead Jct., N.J. (BALL)

EMD division of General Motors has always been *the* diesel builder in the U.S., presently responsible for over 60 percent of the locomotive market. Over the years, train watchers have come to recognize the rounded snouts of EMD passenger diesels as they headed up most of the nation's varnish. At left, three E-8's power the New York-bound *Champion* over the RF&P in Virginia, while below, in a backlit setting, two Burlington E-9's whisk the westbound *California Zephyr* through Lisle, Illinois. At far right, an A-B-B-A F-7 quartet rolls the westbound *Super Chief* out of Shopton (Ft. Madison), Iowa, along the Mississippi River. (BALL, OLMSTED, BALL)

Birds in flight. Flat-faced Alco FA's, in New Haven and Penn Central dress, rush GB-4 west on opposing track, under the wires through Harrison, N.Y., on a warm March day in 1969. At left, a gracious Alco PA passenger diesel leads two snarling GP-9's across the C&O, westbound at Fostoria, Ohio.

At right, in October 1973, the dense surrounding woods of Dunderberg Mountain are obscured in a thick Hudson River fog. It is here that the cold waters of Canopus Creek and Peeks Kill flow down from the hills and into the warmer reach of the Hudson. The rumble of a train can be heard, muffled at first, then a very clear *clickety-clack*. Two snow geese fly low over the water, seconds before an ex-New Haven FL-9 looms out of the murk and bangs across the Peekskill, N.Y., inlet bridge with a Penn Central express from Poughkeepsie. (BALL, HARWOOD, BALL)

In a sense, the scene on the following page shows the first and second generation *hood* units. I was waiting for Pennsy's Proviso transfer run over the C&NW at River Forest, Illinois, when along came a 1,500-h.p. GP-7 on a C&NW local, overtaking the newer 2,500-h.p. GP-35! The "race" was taken in January 1966. (BALL)

Who said all diesels look alike! This random sampling of New York Central diesels should help convince the die-hard students of steam power that there really *is* some variety in diesel-watching. At left, two flashy Alco RS-3's head a Brewster-bound train out of north White Plains, N.Y., while below, the gamut of post-steam diesel power lays over at Harmon, N.Y. At right, a lash-up of New York Central GP-20's sets out cars at Croton, N.Y., terminus of NYC's electric operations. Noticeably absent are the customary dynamic brakes usually found on GP-20's. (BALL)

Erie-Lackawanna's symbol NE-74 cants into the graceful Red Rock curve east of Great Bend, Pa., behind an ensemble that demonstrates the diesel's universal flexibility. The complete diesel dimension is here—from E-8's to SD-45, F-7 and F-3. At the upper left, another cab unit-hood unit combo, this time F-7's and GP-20's, head a New York Central freight up the West Shore, through Iona Island, N.Y., enroute to Selkirk. Below, Pennsy F-7's and GP-30's descend Horseshoe toward Altoona, brakeshoe smoke drifting up behind. (MALINOSKI, WOLFER, YOUNG)

Nothing ordinary in this sampling of some of the more unorthodox diesels and trains that once shared rails with the more common variety of American train. Below, Robert R. Young's BLH-built low-slung Train X (dubbed *Xplorer* on NYC); two GE 8,500 h.p. gas-turbines on the UP (near right); GM's passenger-seeking Arrow Train on the PRR (far right); Alco's big diesel-hydraulic on the SP (below, far right); and German builder Krauss-Maffeis' diesel hydraulic, also on the SP. (BALL)

The bitter and the sweet of it. The decline of the passenger train in America "justified" operating one-car trains, as well as permitting newer power to be assigned to local service. On this page, lone E-8 #825 clips along the Ramapo Valley, with Erie Lackawanna's Port Jervis, N.Y., to Hoboken, N.J., passenger train. Across the Hudson River and on the right, a lone Budd car trundles down the ex-New York Central main, near Cold Spring, N.Y. The cement plant has gone the way of the great steel fleet. Both trains were photographed in March 1974. (BALL)

Super power West! Two brand new 2,500 h.p. Northern Pacific U-25C's run with the wind, approaching Missoula, Montana, from the west on May 15, 1965 (at left). Below, eleven various high-horsepower Southern Pacific units drum out of Colton, Cal., on May 10, 1965, shaking the ground as they head east toward San Gorgonio Pass. It's doubtful, with this lashup, that the helper to Beaumont will be needed! In June 1968, look-alikes SD-40 and SD-45's (far left) approach Donner Summit at the crest of the Sierra Nevada with an SP hotshot. That's Donner Lake, 1,000 feet below. (SMITH, BALL, BALL)

Meet a white elephant! (Lehigh Valley Alco Century 628.) This big fellow exemplifies the crisp appeal so characteristic of Alco. It also commands the respect of Valley crews for being a mountain hauler and is affectionately called "white elephant" by the LV crews. On this page, one of Union Pacific's 5,000 horsepower GE U-50's in portrait, and below, a General Motors 3,600 h.p. SD-45 demonstrator on the otherwise Alco- and GE-powered Delaware & Hudson. All three diesels are representative of today's locomotives, and headed the top of the Alco, GE, and EMD lines when these pictures were made. (BALL)

Railroading today. A Penn Central U-28c leads a parade of power and NG-3 under the former New Haven catenary through Noroton Heights, Conn. The crew has obviously found something the GE engineers most likely overlooked—a niche for their water bottle! At right, in my favorite time of year, Lehigh Valley's big Alco C-628 #639 heads LV-4 through some autumn tapestry near Allentown, Pa. (BALL)

There's no denying that today's diesels have an honest, clean-cut look of utility about them. I find the newest diesels far more pleasing to look at than their earlier hood-unit predecessors. The most familiar of the new diesels are EMD's such as those shown on these pages. In a geographic sampling, we have two GM&O "Red Bird" SD-40's on southbound tonnage through Elwood, Ill., on an extra (above), Santa Fe F-45's heading down the tangent out of Flagstaff, Arizona (at left), and a Chessie GP-40 leading the westbound *Chicagoan* on CNJ rails across the Newark Bay draw (at right). (OLMSTED, BALL, HAND)

On the following pages, the classic Alco PA still reigns on the Delaware & Hudson. The pre-Amtrak *Laurentian* journeys through Willsboro, N.Y., along the beautiful Lake Champlain shore, en route from Montreal. (HAND)

From the chiseled, cowled look of FP-45's and SDP4OF's to the bubble ("beer can") look of Turbo, today's locomotives and self-powered trains are taking on a new "streamlined look" similar to that of previous eras. On the left, and in place of two PA's, a single Santa Fe FP-45 waits on the head end of the *Grand Canyon Limited* for the conductor's highball out of Los Angeles in June 1968. Below, United Aircraft's Turbo Train breezes across the Cos Cob, Conn., draw, while at right, newest-in-the-land SDP4OF's head Amtrak's *Texas Chief* out of Chicago. (BALL)

"Documents of great poignancy." In an intimate physical sense, these classics in black are the absolute embodiment of the three roads that became Penn Central. In these great electric locomotives, we see better days, long since past, on the Pennsylvania, New Haven and New York Central.

Before time takes its toll, on more look at a fast-moving GG-1, (left) whipping a New York bound express through Metro Park, N.J.; At right, a final view of an EP-5, pans lowered, entering third-rail territory at Woodlawn, N.Y., and below, a P-motor loafing along the Hudson with a train for Albany. (BALL)

HAND